F. S. D Ames

Little hinges to great doors

And other tales

F. S. D Ames

Little hinges to great doors
And other tales

ISBN/EAN: 9783741183164

Manufactured in Europe, USA, Canada, Australia, Japa

Cover: Foto ©Andreas Hilbeck / pixelio.de

Manufactured and distributed by brebook publishing software (www.brebook.com)

F. S. D Ames

Little hinges to great doors

Little Hinges to Great Doors

And other Tales.

By F. S. D. AMES,
AUTHOR OF 'MARION HOWARD,' Etc.

LONDON: BURNS & OATES.
1883.

PREFACE.

WE sincerely hope that the appetite of the public for books of this character may continue to grow. Time was, not so long ago, when there was a dearth of intelligent liveliness in English Catholic literature. The effort made by our Catholic publishers to supply the want has had its reward by increasing the demand. Books which, whilst they interest the imagination, also teach the doctrines and practices of the Church will surely find many readers.

The lowliest of principles, which, apprehended, has moved empires, is mysteriously breathed into the minds of men. By what means it reaches this or that mind it is difficult to say; but when the principles of supernatural life are quickening the mind and heart of an intelligent writer, it may well be that the force working so powerfully within should penetrate and influence the quiescent minds of the multitude. So we may hope that these histories of the working of the little seeds of the Gospel in the human heart may stir many young men and women to aspirations above the dead level of ordinary life. Simple as these little histories are, some are true biographies, and tell, what is always interesting to us, the experiences of others' hearts. They show us how in them the principles of Faith, Hope, and Charity struggle triumphantly against the apparently overwhelming weight of worldly influence.

E. L.

CONTENTS.

Faith.

	PAGE
LITTLE HINGES TO GREAT DOORS . . .	1

Hope.

| COUSIN PRUDENCE . . . . . | 99 |

Charity.

| OLD ISAAC'S CHRISTMAS-BOX . . . | 167 |

LITTLE HINGES TO GREAT DOORS

Or 'Ex Ore Infantium.'

CHAPTER I.

ALL ROUND THE FIRE.

IT was an evening in the Christmas week, and a very dismal-looking evening it was too—at least, so thought Miss Margaret Myddleton, otherwise Daisy, as she stood looking out into the twilight through the dining-room window of a pretty house in a West-end suburb of London. Snow had fallen during the day—pretty, white, virgin snow—but it had long since been trodden by hundreds of footsteps into a black unctuous mess, that coated the pavements, and boots of the passers-by, penetrating their soles and worn-out 'uppers' with a spiteful diligence, and sending oftentimes a pang to the very hearts of the wearers. Nor was this all; for overhead there hung, extended like a funereal pall, a yellow, murky, frosty fog that looked almost substantial enough to be cut with a knife or chopped with a hatchet. It was making the old city, at that very moment, a perfect bewilderment of noise and nowhere, smoke and smother, flare and fluster; and if it was not putting suburban pedestrians in actual danger of a violent death, it was doing its best to choke them on the sly by oozing into their mouths and noses, and creeping down their throats into their lungs.

The scene altogether was so dispiriting that Margaret pulled down the blinds and shut the shutters with her own fair hands, and drew the crimson curtains as closely as they could possibly be drawn. She next poked up the fire, and threw on a small beech-log, which flared and crackled until such a glorious blaze was dancing and sparkling in the grate that everything around that could call up a beam danced and sparkled too, and the whole room was flooded with liquid rosy light. For all this, she struck a match to light the gas; but, finding that the maids had not yet turned it on, she gave up the idea, and, taking a large book from the table, drew a stool to the front of the fire, to read in the light and warmth she had created, and shape pictures and stories in the depths of the glowing coals.

Not a word was spoken to break the thread of her fancy tissues, although Daisy was not the only occupant of the room; for, in a large easy-chair by the side of the fireplace, there reposed, in delicious holiday quiescence, her mother's old and valued friend, Father Benedict Stanhope, who had always been their Christmas guest for as many years as Margaret could remember. But Father Benedict (for so he was always called, to distinguish him from his brother, also a priest, and also a friend of the family) had been for an hour past either asleep or at his prayers, she was not quite certain which. But she was quite sure, when she suddenly turned her eyes from her fire-studies, that his face made a very striking picture in the firelight; and she began to consider what a glorious model that fine old head would be for a painter who wanted one for a St. Ambrose or a St. Chrysostom.

When this subject, too, was quite dreamed out, the young lady opened her book, and, drawing nearer to the blaze, began to con over certain plates and sketches of mediæval times contained in the volume, which had just freshly arrived from Mudie's. So deeply absorbed did she become in them that she was altogether unconscious of the fact that a double knock had announced a visitor; and when, later on, two of her younger sisters entered the room, and addressed her, it was not until they had made three successive attempts that they managed to attract her attention.

'Really, Daisy, any one would think you were both blind and deaf,' said Wild-Rose, the youngest child, and, of course, the pet of the family. 'No wonder you were called "Cloudy" at school. I really don't believe you take in one half we say to you.'

'Yes, she does,' said Violet, sidling up to her elder sister; 'or if she does not, it is because she is taking in better things than any we ever say to her; arn't you, Daisy dear? I wish I had been there when the girls called you "Cloudy."' And kneeling down, she nestled her head on Margaret's shoulder.

'What would you have done, Violet?' asked Wild-Rose, quivering all over with fun at the idea of Violet the pacific taking up the cudgels. 'What would you have done?'

A kiss on Margaret's forehead was answer sufficient that, if powerless to repel the injury, Violet would at least have consoled the injured.

'And now, Daisy,' said Wild-Rose, 'I don't expect you know who's here, and has been here for about ten minutes.'

Daisy was obliged to confess that she was in profound ignorance of any arrival whatever having taken place.

'Just like you! Well, guess.'

'I can't,' said Margaret. 'I could never have thought any one would have come out on such a night as this, unless, perhaps, aunt Amy, who has a wonderful knack of turning up just when one least expects her.'

'That is just who it is. She came to Oxford-street on business; but the fog grew so thick that she felt frightened to go back home again, and so jumped into an omnibus and came on to us. Mamma has just sent off a telegram to her uncle to say she is safe, and wants her to stop, now she is here, till next week. I do so wish she would.' And Wild-Rose executed a pirouette that, light as it was, set the glass on the sideboard ringing like a peal of bells.

Now, under the supposition that Father Benedict was asleep, Wild-Rose's share of the conversation had been carried on in an ear-piercing whisper that might have awakened the very heaviest of the Seven Sleepers. That it was gradually rousing him might have been gained from Violet's nervous and often-reiterated 'Hush!' But it was not till he had fairly opened his eyes, at the end of the pirouette, and looked the madcap through and through, that Wild-Rose took in the terrible fact that she was waking Father Benedict—a catastrophe threatened by Mrs. Myddleton with no end of pains and penalties. The situation was so overwhelming that she fled for her life to the door she had left all this time wide open, to be seen no more for the present.

Violet followed with her usual quiet demure step, and, carefully closing the door after her, left the occupants of the dining-room once more in peace and quietness.

'Who is this aunt Amy?' asked Father Benedict, after he had rubbed his eyes well open and taken a pinch of snuff. 'I have been trying to make out, and I cannot; there's no Amy, that I can remember, on either side of the family.'

'O, it is only a name that Wild-Rose gave in fun to Miss Kenrick, a lady about mamma's age, with whom we have become very intimate of late. She is a convert of very many years' standing; but I do not think you have ever met her, father, for she was abroad last year, and the one before we did not know her.'

The entrance of a servant with the tea-tray here put a stop to the conversation; and Daisy went up-stairs to help to welcome aunt Amy. The large bell soon rang, and a few minutes later a bright little party were assembled round that most sociable of all sociable institutions—the tea-table.

They would have made a pretty picture as they sat grouped round that well-furnished table, with its handsome appointments of china and silver, and its store of dainty fare. Very pretty, with the sweet motherly face of Mrs. Myddleton presiding, and the hale, hearty, pious one of Father Benedict saying grace; with aunt Amy in her favourite place at the bottom of the table, more than happy in the unexpected joy of finding herself there, flanked on one side by Violet silent as she was happy, and on the other by Wild-Rose, all chatter and excitement. Nor must we omit Margaret, who—when her head was out of a book—was the very life of the party, and who was now cutting bread, flashing out fun and repartee, and attending to everybody but herself at one and the same time.

Happy hearts, with that substantial partition of bricks and mortar separating them from the slushy snow and murky fog without. Happier still, with that golden barrier of affluence entrenching them beyond the reach of the poverty that was lurking in foodless and fireless homes, not many yards away. Happier than all in the grace of God, that was shielding and protecting them from the vice and iniquity that were blackening, even more deeply than the fog, the great heart of London that night. There was no adjourning to the drawing-room after tea; for, in winter-time, and especially during the absence of Captain Myddleton, the 'state apartment,' as Daisy styled the double drawing-room, was comparatively little used. Not only was the dining-room warmer and snugger, but its large square table was better adapted than the numerous little ornamental ones of the drawing-room to the evening pursuits of a large party. For it must not be supposed that the three young people to whom we have been introduced constituted the whole of Captain Myddleton's family.

Two boys had started that morning for a country visit, and three girls were in a foreign convent, where no Christmas holiday was allowed. That they were not forgotten was testified by Wild-Rose's enumeration of the prizes gained by Burr and Teazle, and Violet's longing loving wish to have her sisters home again.

'This is indeed a Christmas party,' said Mrs. Myddleton, glancing smilingly at the happy faces that surrounded the table.

'Yes,' said Daisy; 'all we want to make it complete is a story.'

'What a capital idea!' exclaimed Wild-Rose; 'who will tell one?'

That was the question. Each one, on being appealed to, declared she was the very worst one in the world to figure as a story-teller; and Father Benedict, whose talents had often been put in requisition on similar occasions, seemed so fast asleep in his favourite corner that even Wild-Rose feared to disturb him.

'I know; let us draw lots,' cried that little lady, so energetically that mamma's finger was raised in warning. 'Let us draw lots,' she repeated, in what she called a whisper; and immediately began to tear a piece of paper into long thin strips, one of which she marked with a cross. Great was the delight of all—save the party interested—when the said pencil cross was found in the hand of Mrs. Myddleton herself.

'But, my dears, you have heard all my stories so many, many times.'

'Not all, mamma; I am sure there must be some we have never heard,' said Violet.

'Let it be a true one, if you can,' put in Wild-Rose; 'made-up stories are more exciting, and all that, but they're not as interesting, after all, as things that have really happened to real people.'

'A true story is it to be?' said Mrs. Myddleton reflectively. 'Well, I will tell you one if you like, but I am afraid Miss Kenrick will find it very uninteresting.'

'O, I am sure she won't! Will you, aunt Amy?'

Of course the lady in question protested that she was quite as anxious to hear the story as the rest of the party.

'There! didn't I tell you so? You see, I am always right!' cried Wild-Rose, so exultingly that Mrs. Myddleton, with a prolonged 'Hush!' pointed warningly to an eye that was opening like an oyster in the large armchair. 'Well, I'll be quiet now, really; I didn't mean to make so much noise. Now, mamma, please begin, or you will not get it finished before supper!'

'One moment, Miss Impatience! I must first find something to do meanwhile, for I am not clever enough to count stitches and talk at the same time. There, now I am ready;' and after clearing her voice in the manner proper to amateur singers, speechifiers, and story-tellers in general, Mrs. Myddleton commenced, greatly to Wild-Rose's satisfaction, in the old-fashioned and orthodox fashion, 'Once upon a time.'

CHAPTER II.

THE PAINTED WINDOW.

ONCE upon a time there was an only child named Clemence, who lived with her parents in an old-fashioned house, in one of the oldest-fashioned villages in England. Mr. and Mrs. Danvers were quiet, simple, easy-going folks, who served God and honoured the king, as their parents had done before them, honest and upright as the day. They cared for little in the world but each other and their child, though they were always ready to extend a helping hand to all who asked them—good, bad, or indifferent, as the case might be.

Of course, I need hardly say they spoiled little Clemence—that is to say, they invariably let her have her own way, and that, of course, is spoiling a child to all intents and purposes. Still, I may add that Clemence loved them both so dearly that I verily believe nothing would have induced her willingly to give them pain for all the world held of toys, sweets, and pleasures added together. I am not, however, going to say that, if it had not been for their sake, Clemence might not sometimes have been very naughty.

One day, when Clemence was about nine years of age, a rather quaint old gentleman called upon Mr. Danvers on business; and, as he was a very old client, the latter asked him to stay to dinner. The invitation was accepted, and Mr. Danvers bustled off at once to find his wife. Nor was this difficult, for his office was in the house, as lawyers' offices often are in the country. After he had told her that Mr. Grant had come, he begged her, if there was time, to order something a little extra nice for dinner; and as Mrs. Danvers thought there was no pleasure in life equal to that of pleasing her husband, she smiled sweetly (instead of frowning as if she wished his friends at Jericho), and promised to do the very best she could.

Now it happened that, on this very morning, Clemence had been allowed to go into the kitchen as a very great treat, to see Martha, the cook, make an apple-pudding for dinner. She was quite disappointed when Jane came down and told Martha that missis wanted her for a minute in the parlour; for the pudding had just arrived at the most exciting part—that is say, the apples were all quartered, and tucked into a sort of paste house in a basin, and only waiting for a round roof to cover them in. Martha returned indeed, as she had promised, in no time, but more like a turkey-cock than the pleasant communicative person she had been all the morning. So cross was she, in fact, that Clemence was too much disconcerted even to notice how the pudding was finished off; and it had actually been dropped, basin and all, into a large black pot on the fire before she even knew that the roof was on. As Martha muttered a great deal about whisking cream and trussing chickens, Clemence dearly longed to stay; but she knew better than to propose any such thing. Nothing ever exasperated the worthy Martha so much as for 'master to go and invite people without giving folks proper warning;' and, although Clemence was only nine years old, she had sense enough to see that the sooner she got out of Martha's way and Martha's kitchen the better.

So she put on her hat, which had been hanging on the chair-back, and started off to the garden. On arriving there, however, the thought came suddenly into her head that she might as well take a peep at the rabbits; and, after gathering some cabbage-leaves, she bent her rapid little footsteps towards the stable-yard. Now, the old horse Blackie had died quite suddenly about six weeks before; and Clemence was very much surprised, on entering the yard, when a familiar hissing sound met her ear, and still more when she saw Tom brushing away at a large white horse on the very spot where dear old Blackie had been rubbed down for so many years.

'O Tom, has papa bought a new horse?'

'No, Miss Clemence, he hasn't, and he ain't likely to neither, I should say, with that 'ere new rally-road a-coming so near that's to take folks everywhere in no time. "Billy," say I, t'other day, to the old stage-coachman, "what will they do with all the hosses when the rally-road comes?" "Kill 'em and eat 'em, I s'pose," says he, "for they won't be of no other manner of use that I can see!" I reckon he's about right, so I do!'

Clemence looked very much disgusted, and puckered up her forehead to consider the subject, but soon dismissed it as beyond her ken.

'Whose horse is it, then?' she asked, as a sudden 'Woa, will ye!' from Tom, again attracted her attention to it.

'It belongs to a gemman that's goin' to stop dinner with the master, and that 'ere is his shay,' he added, pointing to an old-fashioned high-backed gig that was turned down on its shafts in the coach-house. 'My eye! just isn't he a rum old customer! you'd think he'd just walked straight out of Noah's hark. He's never been here afore in my time, but I know who he is.'

'Who?' asked Clemence, opening her eyes wide with curiosity.

'His name's Grant, and he lives about ten miles off, at a large farm called Crossley Hall. And a pretty place it is, too, as you'd say if you was to see it, Miss Clemence.'

'What is it like, Tom?'

'Well, it's a large, big house, rather ramshackly-like, with a flower-garden that's a sight of posies, and a kitchen-garden as big as a field. And then there's orchards upon orchards, and grass-fields and cornfields, and a farmyard filled with stock, and such stock as I never see.'

'Filled with what, Tom?'

'Why, with live-stock, such as cart-horses, and cows, and pigs, and geese, and ducks, and hens, and such sort. Lord love you, that 'ere old gemman and his wife must be as rich as Creases.'

'Have they any children?'

'Never a one; all the better for them as will get their money, say I.'

'And who will have it, Tom?'

'Lord, Miss Clemence, just as if they'd be such fools as to tell! I knows a chap as says it will all go to the Cartholic church down there; for they be Roman Cartholics, so they say.'

'How funny!' said Clemence; 'did you ever go to a Catholic church, Tom?'

'No, Miss Clemence, but that same chap did and he says it's a very grand place indeed.'

'What was it like, Tom ? do tell me!'

'Why, he says it was all full of lighted candles, and flowers, and I don't know what else. And he says there was priests all dressed up most beautiful, in kind of royal robes like, and the music was stunning; and though Bob says the place smoked most awful, the smoke somehow was different to other smoke, and smelt quite good.'

'And does Mr. Grant go to a church like that?' asked Clemence.

'I s'pose he does, for I've always heard tell that he's a Cartholic.'

The conference was here cut short by the appearance of Jane, who had been looking everywhere for Clemence to dress her for dinner, and who carried her off in triumph, with an apron still full of the cabbage-leaves she had not given the rabbits, and her mind full of the strange and wonderful things Tom had just been telling her.

Mrs. Danvers was the soul of punctuality, and everything in her house went as though by clockwork. Just as it struck two, Miss Clemence, arrayed in the whitest of frocks, the bluest of sashes, and the reddest of corals, was led into the dining-room by her mamma, and the instant afterwards they were joined by the gentlemen.

As a rule, often to the vexation of her mother, Clemence was exceedingly shy with strangers, but she was quite at home with Mr. Grant from the moment she first glanced into his eyes, and he into hers. Not only did she offer him her hand with the air of an old acquaintance, but even put up her face to be kissed ; an act of confidence that so charmed the heart of the childless old man, that his eyes glistened beneath his spectacles for nearly five minutes afterwards. When dinner was over she played everything she knew for his amusement, and afterwards brought down all her dolls for his inspection. Great was her delight when she found that he could soon repeat their respective names, and affix them to the rightful owners almost as quickly as she could, and that he took as lively an interest in their personal history as mamma herself. And, strange to say, as she prattled away on his knee, Mr. Grant seemed quite as delighted with Clemence as she undoubtedly was with him. They seemed almost made to be companions, and perhaps there was more affinity between the guileless mind of that childlike old man and the somewhat mature one of the only child, always with grown people, than some might have imagined.

'Papa and mamma are coming over to Crossley Hall to see me next week. Will you come with them, Clemence?' he asked.

'O yes, if they will let me,' answered the child. 'May I, mamma?'

A smile gave consent.

'And come and help the haymakers, eh?' continued the old gentleman. 'O, I forgot. What a pity, it will all be carted by then! Can't you come this week?' he added, turning to Mr. Danvers.

'Impossible. I am very sorry, for Clem would thoroughly enjoy a tumble in the hay-fields.'

'What do you say to my taking her back with me now? Mrs. Grant would be so delighted, and, I am sure I need not say, would take every care of her.'

'What do *you* say, Clem?' asked her father.

To his intense surprise, instead of the emphatic 'No' he had anticipated, no answer at all was returned; but Clemence turned rosy red, and looked up almost wistfully into his face.

'There, there; silence gives consent!' cried Mr. Grant. 'I knew she would like it.'

'Would you really like to go, Clemence?' asked her mother. 'Speak out, darling.'

'Just for a few days, mamma, if you and papa will really come and fetch me; because I couldn't go away for a long time, you know.'

'No, no; they will come in five days, and, if not, I will bring you back myself—I promise you; so run and get your bonnet on, there's a dear,' cried the delighted Mr. Grant.

Although a little more preparation was ne-

C

cessary for the projected journey than the fetching of the said bonnet, by four o'clock everything was ready, and Clemence mounted on the high gig by Mr. Grant's side. Tom, who was holding the horse's head, stood grinning from ear to ear, and more than one happy smile directed at him was intended to convey to her prime favourite Clemence's supreme satisfaction in the fact that she was actually going to realise for herself the wonders he had so graphically described in their late conversation. Only one little drop in her cup of happiness was wanting, and even that was in store for her at the last minute.

Mr. Grant had gathered the reins into his own hand from Tom's, when he suddenly paused and turned to Mr. Danvers.

'How about Sunday, by the bye? I'm afraid the little woman will be lonesome while we are at church; besides, I don't like the idea of leaving her to the servants. I suppose you would not like her to go with us? Afraid of our converting her, eh?'

'Stuff and nonsense!' cried Mr. Danvers. 'She's your child for the next five days. Do what you like with her.'

'She could not be in better hands,' cried the mother, waving her handkerchief as the gig rolled away.

Of course it was only for five days; and yet I feel quite sure, my dear children, if we could have peeped into the drawing-room at that moment, we should have seen two simple pair of eyes quite hazy as they watched that old gig wind away along the turnpike-road.

The delights of Crossley Hall even surpassed Clemence's expectation, seeing that Tom, in his description, had left out a whole piece of ornamental water, with a real boat upon it and two tame swans, and, of course, had not taken the excitement of haymaking into account. Still—for Clemence was a strange child—amid all her happiness, she could not help longing for the intervening days to pass and bring the Sunday, so anxious was she to see with her own eyes the wonderful church. When it arrived at last, and she actually found herself on her way thither, wedged in between the two old people in the high-backed gig, her silent satisfaction knew no bounds.

But, alas for human expectations! If Tom's enumeration of the wonders of Crossley Hall had fallen short of the reality, his account of a Catholic church seemed to have been just as overdrawn, and poor Clemence was bitterly disappointed. It was a poor small mission, and when the priest came out to say his second Low Mass in a simple and somewhat dingy white silk chasuble, Clemence looked in vain for the hundreds of lights, the beautiful flowers, the grand music, and the wonderful smoke. Two little lights there were certainly, and four little vases of flowers; but although at another time these would have amused Clemence as something quite new in a church, what were they after such a description as Tom's?

When Mass was ended, and the candles put out, Clemence thought they were going home; but, to her great disappointment, the priest suddenly reappeared in a simple white surplice, and began to preach. Poor Clemence! if there was one thing she heartily disliked, it was having to sit still during a sermon, and she began to think that, after all, the Catholic church was every bit as uninteresting as her own, except that there was no high green-baized pew to prevent her looking round to count how many children were present, and to see what sort of bonnets the little girls had on.

But, just a few minutes after the sermon commenced, a bright beam of summer sunshine, the first that morning, burst into the church, and suddenly the most beautiful rays of red, green, yellow, and blue began to flicker and dance like fairy fretwork round the place where she was sitting. Instinctively she raised her eyes, and there, high above the altar, was a stained-glass window that Clemence had barely noticed before. Her disappointment—the sermon—all was forgotten as Clemence gazed upon a form of matchless dignity that was rising from an open tomb, while guards fell backward in fear, and angels overhead seemed waving wings of varied hues in triumph. It was the first window of the kind Clemence had ever seen; and even when all was over, and she followed Mr. and Mrs. Grant out of the church, her last look as she turned from the door was a lingering one at the pictured window and its shadow on the sanctuary floor.

Two days later, Mr. and Mrs. Danvers appeared according to promise, and, after spending a pleasant day, returned home in the evening, taking their little Clemence with them.

As weeks and months lengthened into a year the different incidents of her visit grew fainter and fainter in the child's mind, until some altogether faded. But she never forget the painted window; and often when she sat with her parents in the old parish church, in which the Puritan iconoclasts of the sixteenth century had annihilated everything that had once been grand and beautiful, she loved in imagination to fill the old windows with painted panes, and to fancy variegated shadows were dancing on the matted floor.

Mr. Grant had promised to come again for Clemence when the hay-season came next year; but she never went to Crossley Hall again; for, just as the June sunshine was beginning to cap the tall grass with pretty feathery heads, the terrible piece of news was one morning brought in by Tom that dear good old Mr. Grant had died suddenly during the night, and a few minutes afterwards a special messenger rode up to Mr. Danvers's door, begging him to go at once to Crossley. As he said the poor old lady was very ill with the shock, Mrs. Danvers went too, and stayed for several days. Clemence's papa came back at night, but he went again the next day and the next, and so on for the whole week; but, though Clemence felt very lonely at home with only the servants, he never proposed to take her. There was no room for a little girl now in that gloomy house of mourning.

Although Mr. Grant had left a will, there was what people call a legal flaw in it, and, as the responsibility of the said legal flaw rested on Mr. Danvers's shoulders, it worried him terribly, and kept him constantly travelling to and fro between his own house and Crossley. The will was in reality right enough, as was proved in the end; but a bad unscrupulous man thought he saw a chance of getting the main part of the property for himself, and for nearly two years even Mr. Danvers thought the case would go against the dear old widow and certain charitable institutions, to which a great deal of the money had been left.

As long as the summer lasted Mrs. Danvers cared comparatively little for her husband's numerous journeys to Crossley and back; for, contrary to Tom's expectations, his master did buy another horse, and, as it was a fine strong one, she even thought the exercise did him good. During the winter, however, it was a different thing. The road was dark, lonely, and badly kept; and night after night the poor lady trembled at every sound, as she sat expecting him. When, therefore, a second winter found the case still undecided, and a solicitor in the very town where the lawsuit was to be tried signified his intention of giving up his practice, Mr. Danvers, to please his wife, made arrangements to take it, and made her one of the most grateful and happiest little wives in the world.

So the dear old house in the country was given up, and Clemence found herself, for the first time in her life, located in a town; not a large one by any means, for its population only took four figures to represent it; but it seemed a very grand place at first to Clemence, who thought she could never grow tired of looking into the shops or watching the people pass the windows. She was surprised at finding how much smaller it seemed to grow when she knew it well, and had learned the names of all the streets; for it was such a quiet sleepy kind of place that Clemence, who was now twelve years of age, was allowed to go out alone and find her way about from the very first day of their arrival.

One fine bright frosty morning Clemence had

been sent on a little errand by her mother, when it suddenly struck her that a street leading out of the large one she was traversing would very probably be a short cut to the place she wanted. Being naturally of an exploring turn of mind, she at once turned down it, and, strange to say, as she proceeded on her way, although she could not remember when she had been there before, it struck her that she must at some time have seen a certain row of small red almshouses that ran along one side of the road. A little further on she came to a modest building surmounted by a cross; and, as she stood still to look at it, something brought old Mr. and Mrs. Grant so forcibly to her mind, that she gently pushed the door that was ajar still wider open, entered, and stood inside.

Nobody was there but one old woman quietly kneeling at the bottom of the church, near where she stood; and the deserted building looked so different from what Clemence remembered it, crowded with worshippers, that but for the painted window she might not have recognised it. But there the painted window was, bright and beautiful as ever, with its rising Lord, its terrified guards, and its glad triumphant angels. Clemence could not stay long, for she knew that her mother wanted the ribbon for which she had been sent; but when she turned away it was with a happy surging in her heart, as though she had found a dear old friend she had never hoped to see again.

Clemence told her mother of the discovery she had made, but it by no means appeared as important to her as to her daughter. She dismissed the subject with a simple 'Indeed, my dear!' and proceeded to discuss the merits of the ribbon instead. Little did she imagine the chill her apathy had cast over the child's glowing heart, or she would have thrown her whole soul into the matter, and the whole of the ribbon into the fire, if need be, sooner than really pain her darling. But she did not know it, and Clemence shut up her wishings and wonderings in her own heart, or only talked them over with her bosom friend the cat. She was, however, left so far to follow her own devices that when, on the following Sunday, she asked her mother's permission to go and see if there was any service in the church she had told her about, it was at once granted on the simple condition that she should be home before dark.

'I think, my dears,' said Mrs. Myddleton, suddenly breaking off in her narrative, 'some one had better attend to the fire. Put on one of those logs, Daisy, for the fog is really beginning to get into the room. Stories are all very well in their way, but even Wild-Rose would find one a sorry substitute for a fire on such a night as this.'

'Now,' said Wild-Rose, as she once again settled herself after the general move consequent on Daisy's operations with the poker and coal-scuttle, 'now we are getting to what I call the interesting part of the story. Poor little Clemence! I hope she is going to find a nice priest and kind people in that church.'

'I do not suppose, Wild-Rose,' said her mother, 'there ever was a congregation of nicer, kinder people than the one that attended that little church. I have certainly known much grander congregations, but I have never known a more devout one.'

'O, you knew the church yourself mamma, did you? And did you know the priest too?'

'Yes, my dear—but hush! Don't speak so loudly;' and Mrs. Myddleton glanced quite nervously towards the corner where the arm-chair stood.

'No, mamma, I won't; but do tell us what he was like, because so much of the story must depend on that. Of course, I know he was good and holy and zealous, and all that—priests always are; but I mean—well, I mean was he fond of children?' cried Wild-Rose, in an excited key, delighted at finding out what she really did mean.

'Yes, yes, of course—priests always are, especially of noisy ones,' growled a voice from the easy-chair.

To say that Wild-Rose looked startled was no word for the expression of her countenance, while even Mrs. Myddleton seemed disconcerted by the interruption. She found half a dozen little things to do with her handkerchief, her spectacles, and even her brooch, before she recommenced her story. When she did so, it was with more than one nervous glance towards the reverend occupant of the armchair, and in a suppressed voice, that only regained its wonted firmness when Father Benedict showed signs of being again fast asleep.

When Clemence entered the church that Sunday afternoon, she found, to her surprise, that all the front benches were full of children instead of the grown-up congregation she had expected. The priest was hearing them say their Catechism, and Clemence crept quietly into a place near the bottom of the church, where she sat drinking in every word of question and answer, and thinking how frightened she should feel, if she were among those children, when she heard the sound of her own voice. Benediction always followed the Catechism; and as Clemence sat in her quiet corner, watching everything, all that Tom had told her that morning in the stable-yard floated through her mind. With it came quite a feeling of disappointment that he should have gone to America, and that she should never now have the chance of telling him that she had seen, with her very own eyes, all that had seemed so extraordinary to them both in his friend Bob's recital. For there were the tiers of lighted candles, and the large handsome vases of flowers; there, too, were the gorgeous robes (for certainly the little church possessed both a handsome cope and humeral veil); there, too, was music, grander and sweeter than any Clemence had ever heard before; there was even the strange aromatic smoke curling and circling high over the priest's head till it obscured the painted window, when it broke, and dispersed into fragrant clouds that crept softly and slowly down the church to the very bench where Clemence, awed through and through, was sitting.

Sunday after Sunday, Clemence went to St. Joseph's Church, creeping nearer and nearer to the children each time, until she almost reached the last of the three benches they occupied. But there she stopped, hiding her slim little figure behind them, and never attempting to mingle with the ranks. Perhaps she felt instinctively that, even if she were with them, she would not be of them, though how much she longed to be part and parcel of that little company only her own heart and pussy ever heard. Supposing some day, by some lucky chance—she could never imagine what—she should take her place as one of that row of happy girls? The thought was simply overpowering. Meantime she kept her distance like a humble little dog, rejoicing over, if not content with, the crumbs that fell from the Master's table. It may be the desire was the stronger from the circumstance that Clemence, who was taught at home, had never in her life had other children for companions.

She was standing one day at the window, thinking of all these things, when she suddenly espied an old woman, with a basket on her arm, stop at their front door; and, just as she rang the bell, Clemence recognised the form and features of the very Irishwoman she had so often seen at her prayers at the bottom of the church. When Martha went to open the door, Clemence, almost sick with the intensity of her curiosity, stood behind in the passage to listen.

'Any boot-laces to-day, child?'

'No!' was the curt reply; and Martha, who was in one of her very worst humours, was about to slam the door.

Clemence darted forward with cheeks so red, and eyes so bright with excitement, that even Martha was almost surprised out of her sulks to ask what was the matter.

'Stop a minute, Martha, I want one. Let me have a boot-lace; here's a penny,' she added, springing to the door with such impetus that she knocked against Martha, who walked off angrier than ever to the kitchen. 'At least, that is to say, if a penny is enough,' she added, speaking in a very respectful tone to the old woman.

'Enough, is it? Bless your heart, child, you can have two of the likes of that sort for a penny.'

'This kind will do,' said Clemence, as she handed her the coin. She took the laces from the old woman's hand so mechanically as she spoke, and looked so eagerly up into her face, that it was evident to the latter that other business had yet to be transacted, and, standing her basket down on the step, she, in her turn, looked inquiringly at the little lady.

'You go to the Catholic church, don't you?' asked Clemence; 'I am sure I have seen you there.'

'I do, darlint; glory be to God!'

'Do you know the gentleman who hears those children say their lessons—I mean their Catechism?'

'Is it the priest you mane? Sure, thin, and haven't I known him since he was that high, God bless him?'

'Do you think, if any one he knew was to ask him, that he would let me say my Catechism with those children?'

'Indade, and it's meself will ax him. But you're not a Catholic, honey, or you'd have larned it long since!'

'No; I'm not a Catholic, and I don't know a word of it yet; but I would soon learn it if he would let me. I would ask mamma to buy me a book.'

'Here's a book for you, and welcome,' said the old woman, suddenly producing a little green Catechism from under her other wares.

'O, thank you, very much!' cried Clemence, her eyes sparkling with delight; 'tell me how much it is, and I'll fetch—'

'Whisht, child, whisht! Nothing at all. Ould Biddy can afford that much for the love of God and His Blessed Mother. You just look out for me in the chapel, birdie, next Sunday afternoon, and I'll take you to his riverence myself!'

The very next Sunday, when Clemence made her appearance in the church, the old woman beckoned her forward, and told her that the priest was expecting her in the sacristy. Everything seemed to swim around her as she made her way up the side aisle to the spot in question, and it was an intense relief when she discovered that old Biddy had followed in her wake, and was standing close beside her.

'Is this the little girl you were telling me about, Biddy?' He looked so kindly at Clemence as he spoke, and took her hand in his, that she felt quite reassured.

'It is, your riverence,' said Biddy, making a profound obeisance, which Clemence immediately did her best to imitate. The funny twinkle in the eyes that met hers, as she stood erect after her 'bob,' made Clemence feel more at home with him than ever.

'And so you want to learn Catechism, do you? But you are not a Catholic?'

'No, sir.'

'Then why do you want to learn the Catholic Catechism?'

The child was silent, but he had penetration enough to see that the superabundance rather than the paucity of her reasons embarrassed her.

'Try and tell me.'

'Because I so love to hear all you say to the children, and I want to learn and know all these things my very own self.'

'Your parents are living?'

'O yes, yes,' said Clemence, shuddering even at an idea to the contrary. 'I am sure I should be dead too if they were.'

'And what will they say to your learning our Catechism?'

'Nothing. I told mamma before I came out that I was going to speak to you about it, and she said I might do whatever I liked, as long as I did not stay too long, and only sat with clean respectable children.'

'You shall certainly do that. But your parents must have great confidence in you.'

'Yes they have,' said Clemence simply, 'but

it is because they are so good that if I were even ever so bad they would know I could never find it in my heart to do anything to grieve them; and so of course they trust me, and almost always let me do what I like.'

'Happy child! happy parents!' said the priest musingly. 'Well, I will give you a Catechism, and show you what to learn.'

'Thank you, sir, but I have one already, that Mrs.—Mrs. Biddy gave me, the day she came to our house.' (I may here add that Bridget Noonan went by the name of Mrs. Biddy for many a long day afterwards at the presbytery.) 'I have learned the Lord's Prayer, because that was the only thing I knew in it.'

'And so you learned it for that reason?' and a pair of comical eyes looked so funnily at her, that Clemence laughed almost merrily.

'I mean, sir, it was the only one thing I had ever been taught in the whole book, and so I learned all the Catechism said about it, and I quite understand it now.'

'I see,' said the priest, looking more kindly than ever into the eager eyes before him. 'Very well, my child, go now and take your place among the others. The clock is just striking three. You can go and show her where to sit, Mrs. Biddy.'

Proud alike of the joke and the charge, Biddy

made her way to the Catechism class, and, after seeing that Clemence made what she considered a proper genuflection before the altar, deposited her in triumph in the very front row. This accomplished, and throwing up both eyes and hands in gratitude to heaven, she bent her steps to her usual place at the foot of the great crucifix at the bottom of the church.

You, my dear children, who know so well that between the paper covers of a penny Catechism sufficient theology is contained to take the wisest man that ever lived to heaven; and you who know, moreover—thanks be to God!—how earnestly our priests instruct the lambs of the fold, will not be surprised to hear that by the end of a month Clemence was thoroughly instructed in all the leading doctrines of the Catholic Church. So little, however, did her parents think of it that when, one Sunday afternoon, on returning home, she drew her stool to the front of the sofa on which her parents were sitting, and asked them, in the simplest manner possible, to let her become a Catholic, both Mr. and Mrs. Danvers were very much surprised indeed.

'Bless my heart, Clem!' cried Mr. Danvers, 'what a very extraordinary idea! A Catholic! Why, my child, you know nothing at all about them. I don't suppose you ever spoke to one in your life except the Grants, poor things!'

'Yes, she has, my dear. Clemence has been going a great deal lately to their church. She asked me to let her go, and I said yes, as a matter of course. I never dreamed that anything like this could possibly come of it, or I certainly would have spoken to you about it— you know I would, Reginald;' and the poor little woman glanced up into her husband's face with almost a frightened look in her eyes.

'Of course not, my dear; how could you guess such a thing?' said Mr. Danvers soothingly, and at the same time patting her hand to reassure her. 'But I am sure Clemence does not mean what she is saying.'

'Yes, I do, papa. Do say yes, dear papa, please!'

'But a Catholic, Clemence — a Roman Catholic! It is such a very extraordinary thing to ask. Why, child, there never was such a thing heard of in the family before.'

'O yes, papa, there must have been indeed. Three hundred years ago, you know, there was no other religion, and both mamma's and your great-great-great-great-grandfathers and grandmothers must have been Catholics. So I should only go back, you see, to the old, old religion, after all.'

'Well, granting you are right, three hundred years is a long way to go back for a precedent. We shall have you bothering your mother for an Elizabethan ruff, or me for a cast of hawks, next.'

'No, you won't, papa. I only mean to ask you for just this one simple thing—don't say no, papa, please!'

'But, my child, you will have to confess your sins, half starve yourself, and goodness knows what. Now, do be sensible, and ask for something else instead, Clem. We really cannot give way to you in this.'

'I shall be really very, very unhappy unless you do.' And real, large, briny tears stood in Clemence's eyes as she spoke.

The parents looked at each other in positive alarm.

'Well, run along and play, and come back to us in five minutes,' said the father, after a pause.

Never had five minutes, which were counted exactly by the old clock on the stairs, seemed so long. The instant they were over, Clemence sped to the drawing-room.

'Well, papa—well, mamma—may I?'

'Is your happiness really so much involved in this wild idea, Clemence?' asked the latter, drawing her to her side and kissing her.

'Yes, mamma. I shall never be happy again if you say no.'

'Then we will not say no,' said Mr. Danvers. 'You shall do as you like. I don't very much care. You will soon grow tired of it, I know.'

Clemence's eyes and Clemence's heart said she should do no such thing; but her only answer to her father was a kiss.

The following Sunday Clemence again took up the same position, and sat looking, with a strange happy expression, into the loving eyes that smiled down into hers.

'And when are you going to take this important step, Clem ?' asked Mr. Danvers, pulling her hair. 'When are you going to be made a Roman Catholic ?'

'I am one already, papa.'

'The deuce you are ! Why, Clem, what did they do to you ?'

'Baptised me conditionally, for one thing.'

'Baptised you !' cried both parents together.

'That was done when you were only a month old,' added Mr. Danvers.

'Of course it was,' chimed in his wife, quite indignantly.

'Yes, I know ; but I only said conditionally. That means in case it wasn't properly done then, you know.'

'Properly done ! I like that !' exclaimed Mr. Danvers. 'It was very properly done indeed, Clem. The old General and his wife stood godfather and godmother, and, what was better still, she stood a handsome silver knife, fork, spoon, and goblet, and he put a 50*l*. note in the bank for you. If ever a child had a proper christening you had, and that I can answer for, Miss Clem.'

Instead of disputing the question, Clemence bent down to stroke the cat.

'I know what I wish,' she said at length, glancing up at them with the arch expression of a loving yet sadly-spoiled child.

'What is it now, you monkey?'

'That you and mamma were both Catholics.'

'Much obliged to you. Perhaps you would like me to wear trunk hose, too, by way of a change?'

'No, I shouldn't, because the name sounds ugly, and I always like to see you and mamma in things that are pretty and nice. But I really mean what I say. You would be so happy,' persisted Clemence.

'Are we not happy now?' asked the mother, somewhat reproachfully.

'O yes, mamma, of course; very, very happy,' and Clemence kissed her mother almost passionately; 'but sometimes, you know, even happy people get suddenly unhappy, like the Edensons.'

The family she mentioned had suffered such an utter wreck of a bright and happy home that Mr. and Mrs. Danvers seemed almost brought suddenly face to face with death and misfortune.

'But how would they have been happier in their terrible troubles if they had been Catholics, Clem?'

'Because, papa, then they could have gone to church and forgotten them. I do so wish you and mamma would go to Catechism just once to please me.'

'Really, Clem, you are growing too *exigeante*. I cannot consent to give up one of my precious Sunday afternoons even for your sake.'

'Not just for once, papa? Not if I ask prettily and say please?' and Clemence's head fell on one side, as it always did when she begged very hard for anything.

'No; I really cannot, Clem.'

'Yes, you can, and you must! I have just remembered! Next Sunday will be my birthday, and I choose *that* for my treat instead of anything else. So now you are caught; isn't he, mamma?'

Of course he was, and so was Mrs. Danvers; for to refuse anything to Clemence, when she had chosen it for a birthday treat, would have been indeed an innovation—a proceeding altogether unprecedented in the history of the household.

I need hardly say that when Mr. and Mrs. Danvers made their appearance at the church next Sunday afternoon, no witch was needed to tell his reverence who they were. It may easily be imagined, too, how kindly he received them, what a comfortable seat he found for them, and how he made the children show off to the best possible advantage. When Benediction was over a little boy was sent to the bench where they sat, to say the priest would be with them almost immediately; and when, a few minutes after, he made his appearance, it was to invite them into his house. Once there, he easily induced them to stay tea with him, and sent Mrs. Danvers and Clemence straight up-stairs with his dear old housekeeper to take off their bonnets.

They came down, to find Mr. Danvers and their host in the midst of an animated conversation. The former had discovered in the latter the son of an eminent barrister, and discovered, too, to his delight that the priest remembered so much about the circumstances attending the various *causes célèbres* that had made his father famous, that it was almost as good as talking to the old counsellor himself. As Mrs. Danvers soon became equally interested, they spent a most delightful afternoon till the bell tolled out for evening service, and even then, instead of going home as Clemence expected, to her great delight they walked into the Catholic church instead. Certainly the Vespers were not chanted by the little country choir in first-rate style. Still, the good old tones always sound well, and the sermon that followed was so practical and sensible, and eloquent withal, that Mr. Danvers was delighted, and pronounced on it the highest praises in his power by dubbing it 'worthy of the father's son.'

Their visit to the presbytery was not only returned, but returned with interest, and many a spare hour did his reverence devote to his new friends, and they on their side grew so much attached to him that they soon learned to look forward with eagerness to his visits. Now, although the son of the Q.C. loved to talk over the triumphs of his father on earth, the one dear object of his consecrated life was the interests of his Father in heaven, and we may be quite sure they were not forgotten in his conversation with Mr. and Mrs. Danvers. Insensibly one article of faith after another was introduced and explained, but so modestly and quietly was it done, that it never struck Mr. or Mrs. Danvers that either was being converted.

But they were converted nevertheless, and were received into the Church about six weeks after their little daughter; just in time to enjoy as Catholics, the sweet solemnities of Holy Week and Eastertide. On Whit-Sunday they all three made their first Communion; and never were there, I will venture to say, three happier people in the world than that father, mother, and little daughter on that bright glad day of Pentecost.

What was better still, they persevered, two of them, we may hope even to the end. For at a good old age, when Clemence's children had grown almost as dear to them as Clemence herself, Mr. and Mrs. Danvers passed away almost at the same time; both thanking God, like the great St. Teresa, that they were children of the Church.

'And Clemence, mamma; what of her? did she marry a Catholic?'

'Yes, my dear; a good, earnest, devoted Catholic, and had a large family of sons and daughters.'

'And were they all as good as she was?'

'No,' said a deep voice from the corner. 'She had a certain daughter named Wild-Rose, who was the very plague of her life, and of everybody else's too, for the matter of that.'

'O Father Benedict! Wild-Rose? That's me! What, has mamma been telling us her own story?'

'She has.'

'I should never have ventured to do so, father,' observed Mrs. Myddleton, 'but I really thought you were fast asleep.'

'Never a wink. Heard every word of it—even down to the "comical eyes." By the bye, I must have a look at them;' and Father Benedict jumped up and gravely contemplated himself in the glass.

'O Father Benedict, what fun! Were you the priest?' asked Wild-Rose, laughing heartily. 'Well, they say listeners never hear any good of themselves, but I am sure you have heard a great deal this evening.'

The yellow fog rolled away in the night—whither, we know not. Whether it swept northward to the great bleak moors, westward to the mountains, or southward to the wolds, or whether it crept into the fens or marshes of the East, or along the Thames, to float away in a cloud across the German Ocean, we cannot tell ; but certain it is it did go somewhere, and let the winter sunshine next morning gleam so brightly, and the fresh frosty breezes blow so merrily, that London rejoiced in her heart and was glad.

Tempted out by the beauty of the weather above, people recked little of the mud that still lay below, and a long pent-up tide of pedestrians again appeared in the highways and byways—ladies, invalids, children, nurses, and perambulators. As these, for the most part, wore their brightest Christmas faces, and the shops one and all displayed their brightest Christmas wares, the scene presented that day throughout the width and breadth of our grand old metropolis must have been a very bright one indeed.

Mrs. Myddleton, Daisy, and aunt Amy had started on a shopping excursion directly the early dinner was over ; but, as the younger girls had colds, it had been judged advisable, sorely against their will, that they should not only keep to the house, but even as much as possible to the genial atmosphere of the dining-room. They were soon, however, cheered up by the return of Father Benedict, who had taken his constitutional in the morning; and while he sat and read in his favourite corner, they stitched away at certain dolls they were dressing for a school-feast, making such fashionable trains and tunics for the waxen belles that Wild-Rose almost envied them her own handiwork. Of course, as usual, she chatted and prattled nineteen to the dozen; while Violet, quite as happy in her way, plodded silently on, stitching, snipping, measuring, and admiring, quite content to leave the talking part of the business to her sister.

'O, what a funny little man!' cried Wild-Rose, suddenly springing up from her seat and hastening to the window; 'do come and look at him, Violet!'

'I cannot, my dear; if I were to lay down this trimming, I should never get it right again.'

'What a nuisance! I do so wish you could see him. I never saw such a queer-looking little fellow. He has a very large head, with the funniest-looking little hat upon it you ever saw; and his eyes remind me of that old god what's-his-name's, which they say were a day's journey apart. He is walking with an old lady, and takes as much care of her as if she were a baby.

Why, Violet, they are actually standing still and looking across at this house. And now, I declare,' continued Wild-Rose, with increasing excitement, 'they are beginning to cross the road, though she is so afraid of the carts and carriages, I don't believe he will ever get her over. Surely they cannot be coming here ?'

'Not very likely,' said Violet. 'We know nobody, I am sure, at all answering to the very unflattering description you have given of the poor gentleman.'

'They are, though; for he is opening the gate already. What shall we do, Violet? I never shall be able to keep serious and talk to such a dreadful little man as that.'

'He cannot be very dreadful, Wild-Rose, if he is so kind to his old mother.'

'He is nice certainly in that one thing, but he is very dreadful in everything else. Hark! there now, he is knocking. Who can he be?' and Wild-Rose hurried to the door, and opened it a little way to listen.

The voice that spoke at the front door was, however, so nicely modulated that Wild-Rose strained her ears in vain, and at last closed the door of the room in disgust and returned to her place.

'Some Mr. Jones or Smith wanted, I suppose,' she said half-crossly as she took up her needle.

'If you please, father, a lady and gentleman wish to see you if you are disengaged,' said Ann the housemaid, suddenly entering the room; 'Mr. and Mrs.—'

'I know,' said the priest. 'Thank you, my child. Say I will be with them immediately;' and, laying down his book, he walked out of the room.

Wild-Rose looked the picture of consternation.

'O Violet, what shall I do? Who could have thought that funny little man could turn out to be a friend of Father Benedict's? O my dear, do you think he heard what I said?'

Father Benedict's ears were so very sharp that Violet could only shake her head dubiously.

'Will he be very angry, do you think?'

Again the shake of the head; for Violet knew well that Father Benedict especially disliked any form of 'making fun,' and had been very severe on certain similar occasions.

'Will he speak to mamma and get me into disgrace, do you suppose?'

The thought was terrible; but Violet, not knowing what might happen in consequence of her sister's indiscretion, could only get up and twine her arms round Wild-Rose's neck to comfort her beforehand in case of the worst.

Father Benedict's visitors remained about an

hour. The sound of his voice dismissing them in the hall brought Wild-Rose's heart into her mouth, and, had it not been for her mother's injunction to remain in the warm room, she certainly would have made her escape up-stairs. But her obedience chained her to the spot, and she sat and awaited Father Benedict's return, sick at heart, and silent as Violet herself. But not a word did he say beyond a remark that the air was beginning to feel frosty again; after which, and a vigorous poke at the fire, he resumed his seat and his book, and was once again as deep in the latter as ever.

The girls were only just recovering their spirits when Mrs. Myddleton's return again threw a damper over them, so afraid were they both that Father Benedict's wrath might, after all, only have been bottled up and reserved till now. But he greeted the little party warmly and brightly as usual, and at tea-time was even more cheerful and talkative than he had appeared for days. If he had heard Wild-Rose's remarks, it became so evident to her that he had forgotten them that she began to forget them too, and speedily became her own wild little self again, the madcap of the party.

But, agreeable as Father Benedict had shown himself over tea, it was nothing to what he had yet in store for them. When the various evening occupations were arranged and commenced, he seemed quite to expand with the occasion. Instead of retiring to his usual corner, he drew a chair to the table, where he sat, cutting funny little jokes as fast as Mrs. Myddleton cut out funny little pinafores for the infant-school. He resumed his ordinary manner after a time, but each member of the little party felt, as he chatted with them, that a calm quiet happiness pervaded every word and action. At length he put the finishing-stroke to his complacency, by asking Wild-Rose if she would like a story.

'Very much, father; is it to be a true one?'

'Yes,' said the priest, with an unwonted solemnity in his tone and a strange light shining in his eyes, 'a true one; he whose history I am going to relate to you is as dear to the heart of Father Benedict as any who are assembled around this table to-night.'

CHAPTER III.

THE STEPMOTHER.

MANY years ago there was a young lady named Adelaide, very pretty, lively, and sweet-tempered, but, unfortunately, poor child, for herself and others, too fond of the world, and sadly deficient in what we may call the ballast of religious principles. Yet it ought not to have been so; for Adelaide was a Catholic, and had been carefully trained in her childhood by a very pious mother. But God had seen proper to remove that mother when Adelaide was still quite young, and she had been thrown, in consequence, a great deal into worldly society. Little by little its maxims had crept into her mind, and just in proportion, though Adelaide continued to practise her religion, its precepts lost their proper place in her heart and their hold upon her conscience.

Adelaide's father had been considered a rich man; and she had always found herself so surrounded by comforts and luxuries that she had learned to reckon them among the very necessaries of life. When, therefore, upon the merchant's sudden death his affairs were found to be upon the verge of bankruptcy, and it was proved beyond a doubt that nothing but a miserable pittance would remain for this spoiled and petted child, Adelaide nearly collapsed. It might have been pointed out to her that the poverty, the holy poverty that stood ready to embrace her, was God's own darling daughter. But *cui bono?* One might as well describe a colour to the blind, or music to the deaf, as to talk of either the holiness or happiness of poverty to a worldly soul knowing nothing of resignation, and having no trust in God.

She fell ill, so ill that a friend removed her to a fashionable watering-place for change of air. The sea-breezes once more restored the roses to her cheek; but what was that to her if they were only to bloom in the obscurity of straitened means? The roses, however, were not destined for that; they attracted instead the attention of a gentleman of position, who made her an offer of marriage; and although Adelaide knew well that he professed no religion at all, she at once accepted him.

Her mother's old confessor, Father Bernard, chancing to hear the news, hastened over to expostulate with her; but to no avail. To all his representations of the misery she might expect if she persisted in this marriage she opposed a doleful picture of the penury that awaited her if she kept single. Sweet as was her manner to her mother's old friend, her sweetness was fully equalled by her obstinacy, and the only satisfaction Father Bernard gained by his visit was a flippant verbal promise from the gentleman that Adelaide and any children she might have should be free to practise the Catholic religion.

And so Adelaide was married, and as Mrs. Ainslie took a higher place than ever in the grand world—carriages, servants, a costly house and furniture, jewels, and rich attire, all were hers. When, in due time, two children—a boy and a girl—came successively to gladden her heart, she probably counted herself one of the happiest women in the world. 'I go regularly to church, and my children are both baptised Catholics. What more could I have had,' she wrote and asked Father Bernard, 'if I had married the most zealous Catholic in the world?'

'A great deal more,' he answered, 'if only in the daily intercourse of one child of God with another, by no means the smallest prerogative of the Sacrament of Matrimony.'

And bitterly Adelaide answered the question herself, when, ten years after her marriage, her mother's malady showed its symptoms, and grave physicians announced that Mrs. Ainslie was in a decline. Recovery was hopeless, one good old man gently hinted; and Adelaide, who understood him, lay, and looked just as angrily and unresignedly at death as she had once looked at poverty, with just the same wild clinging to the world and the things of the world as then.

But once again Father Bernard heard the news, and, though a very old man now, once again he came to the rescue. And by the grace of God his words this time took effect, as he talked of peace and pardon, heaven and God; and long before death really came, Adelaide had learned to love the thought of its coming. Indeed, so deep was her love, so earnest her contrition, that I believe if God had willed her to rise from that sick-bed, Adelaide Ainslie would have been thenceforth a model Catholic in every relation of life. But it was not so ordained.

But it was ordained that now, notwithstanding her new-found happiness, Adelaide should drain the very dregs of the bitter cup the old priest had foretold ten years before. Now did she realise for the first time her responsibility as a Catholic mother. Now was it that her husband's want of religious principle—the very thing that had hitherto made her course so easy —became her terror day and night. Much as Mr. Ainslie had always loved her, and fairly as he promised now, what reliance could she place on the word of a man who, professing no religion, scoffed at each in turn. Did she not know, from daily observation, how soon the wishes of the dead are forgotten? Did she not know furthermore, after her years' experience of his character, that if the conversion of his children to Islamism or Judaism would promote his temporal advantage or theirs, he would just as willingly hand them over to an Imaum or a Rabbi as to a Catholic priest? Had not Father Bernard himself been only treated with the barest possible civility for her sake? and did she not see, with a clearness akin to prescience, that after her death his visits to the house would be expected to cease? Who or what was there, then, to reassure her that her little ones should be reared in that faith that at this her eleventh hour had become their mother's all in all?

Possessing none but distant relations, one hope alone remained to the dying woman. Among the few Catholics she knew was a certain Miss Trevor, a person of no position whatever in society, but whose acquaintance Mrs. Ainslie had made through her repeated calls at her house on begging expeditions. Now, this Miss Trevor had been notorious at one time, in her own circle of acquaintances, as an arrant flirt and fortune-hunter, but, meeting with a terrible disappointment, she had subsequently taken to piety in lieu of her usual pursuits. After passing through all the many gradations of Low Church, High Church, and Ritualism, she had, two or three years before, become a Catholic, and as such had made a very great show of her new religion. And certainly, if talking of nothing but priests and nuns, confraternities, sermons, missions, and the Lord knows what, be religion, Miss Trevor was a very religious person indeed. Her principal *attrait* at that time, I should say, was herself, but she informed her friends it was for nursing the poor. This *attrait* she followed with so much devotion, up and down courts and alleys where she could be seen of men and women, that for the home-circle, where she was not seen, she had no time to spare, and her poor aged mother had to pay a hireling to minister to her necessities. In fact, as I look back, Miss Trevor's works of charity seem to me to have been very much like that celebrated representation of the play of *Hamlet,* in which Hamlet himself was left out. Poor dear soul, were she with us here to-night, I would say precisely what I am saying now; and I am certain she would see, in her sweet humility, that this picture of her is not one whit overdrawn, for certainly in those days Louisa Trevor was one of the foolish virgins.

But Mrs. Ainslie knew nothing of all this; thoroughly sincere herself, she believed in everybody else's sincerity. Cut off for years from all intercourse with really devout persons, to her inexperienced eye Miss Trevor's numerous gyrations round the parish, and her sonorous mouthing of pious platitudes, appeared genuine love of God and zeal for souls. When it therefore became a question of choosing some person to watch over her children's faith, Mrs. Ainslie sent for Louisa Trevor, and earnestly besought her to accept the solemn charge, and never to abandon it unless forced to do so by circumstances impossible to control.

Only too delighted with the *éclat* of the responsibility, and only too proud of the power about to be vested in her, Miss Trevor gave the required promise; then and there adding so many pretty words by way of accompaniment that the poor weary head fell in gratitude on her shoulder, and the poor tearful eyes smiled happily into her own. But old Father Bernard, who was present at the conference, by no means found himself as pleasurably affected. On the contrary, he was secretly very much dissatisfied with the poor mother's choice. As, however, he could not propose any one in whom Mrs. Ainslie seemed to feel so much confidence, he said nothing on the subject. But that Father Bernard had a presentiment of evil, as that awful promise rolled so glibly from Louisa Trevor's lips, I have often heard him say.

Mrs. Ainslie passed away almost directly after, blessing her children with her latest breath, and with her dying eyes begging her husband to remember his promise. Before a week had elapsed Miss Trevor made her appearance at the house of mourning, to enter upon her duties, or rather what she chose to consider her duties, to the orphaned children. Anxious as Mrs. Ainslie had been to provide against any attempt that might be made, sooner or later, against the religion of her children, she had certainly never contemplated the remotest chance of any immediate interference on her husband's part. Their mutual affection had left no place for any such idea, and she had only feared for the time when that affection should have lost its hold upon him. She had, moreover, explained so clearly to Miss Trevor, in Father Bernard's presence, exactly what she did fear, that it never entered into the mind of either of them that that lady would attempt any interference with the existing arrangements of the household, and base that interference upon Mrs. Ainslie's dying request. But they little knew Louisa Trevor. No half-measures for her! Whatever she undertook must be done thoroughly, &c. To the disgust of the good old Irish nurse who had tended the little Hubert and Emmeline from their birth, and instilled into their hearts her own ardent faith—as a fervent Irish Catholic always does instil it—the children were now demanded, in their mother's name, 'to be taught their religion.' What was worse still, the delicate little ones were dragged out, on raw misty mornings, to early Mass, and kept out late on foggy afternoons at Benediction; while their brains were taxed at any hour of the day that Miss Trevor chose for her 'instructions,' without regard to their meals, walks, or anything else whatever but her own whim or fancy at the moment.

As might naturally be expected, old Nana was simply furious at the appearance of this interloper on her territory; and the worst of it was she could devise no means of redress. Had Mr. Ainslie been a Catholic she would at once have carried her complaints to him; but knowing, as she did, how entirely the religion of her darlings was a thing of sufferance, she felt that she must be prepared to endure anything and everything rather than put that sufferance in jeopardy by an ill-timed complaint. But to what an extent that Irish blood of hers bubbled and boiled at the impertinent interference of a stranger nobody but herself knew.

When, however, Miss Trevor, elated by her success in the nursery, attempted to introduce certain reforms into other departments of the household, she by no means found the rest of the servants as forbearing as Nana, the only Catholic one in the house. They, at least, were not going to stand it, they declared from the outset; and that very night, on returning home, Mr. Ainslie found a deputation awaiting him from the kitchen, in the portly person of the cook, who informed him, on the part of every servant in the house, that they were not 'a-going to stand that there Miss Trevor's ways for no one.'

The result was a conference between Mr. Ainslie and the lady in question the very next morning, at which, he being a fine gentlemanly man, and she—in spite of her semi-religious disguise—a very handsome woman, they became mutually pleased with each other. One conference led to another; and although the indignant domestics found so little redress from any of them that they all left Mr. Ainslie's service except the old nurse, Miss Trevor soon saw reason to believe that these conferences would quickly lead to a very satisfactory result to her. Little by little her whole course of life was changed: her dress was modified; the courts and alleys saw her no more; and when, just a year after his wife's death, Mr. Ainslie led her up to the altar of her own church, and married her in the sight of the congregation, though every member of it felt shocked and scandalised, nobody was astonished.

During the six weeks of the honeymoon the absence of her late tormentor left Nana free to follow the rules of her old mistress, and to order the children according to her lights, just as in the good old days. But it was an anxious time with her, for all that; for it was not a pleasant thing to reflect that this reversor of all system and order was now, by the law of the land, her own mistress, and, what was worse still, stepmother to her darlings. Look at the question as she might, only two alternatives lay before her in the dark future—that of instant compliance with any amount of foolish and injurious whims, or separation from those who were far dearer to her loving old heart than life itself.

But the anticipation of evil is often worse than the evil itself; and it certainly was so in this instance. Mrs. Ainslie launched in her airy pinnace among the gilded craft of the upper ten thousand was a very different person from Miss Trevor steering her single bark, as best she might, in search of a desirable haven. Calling, driving, riding, dinner-parties, and balls took the place of her late pious pursuits; and certainly visits to the nursery of her stepchildren found no place in the new Mrs. Ainslie's programme.

This was, of course, highly satisfactory to Nana; but she was even better satisfied when an unforeseen circumstance suddenly removed both herself and her nurslings from the house, and put hundreds of miles between them and their new stepmother. The representative of the elder branch of Mr. Ainslie's family was Lord Grosvenor Mount-Maurice—an old nobleman, religious according to his lights, but very vain of his oratorical powers, and very fond of airing them in public. He and his wife had been for many years in the habit of sojourning in London during the 'May meetings' at Exeter Hall, but had invariably remained aloof from Mr. Ainslie's house on the score of the late Mrs. Ainslie's religion.

Hitherto Mr. Ainslie had taken no trouble to ingratiate himself with his noble kinsman. For years only one man had stood between himself and the Mount-Maurice estates, alienable and inalienable; but that man had been a fine young cousin, whose robust health had seemed to promise him a long term of life. But this promising son and heir had been quite lately killed in the hunting-field, leaving an only boy, puny and sickly in the extreme, to inherit his expectations. Affairs were now on a different footing, and Robert Ainslie came to the conclusion that it was high time to court the old gentleman's favour and good opinion. His new wife's religion had not yet transpired; and Mrs. Ainslie, who well understood the meaning of alienable property, and who, from the day of her marriage, had earnestly desired to propitiate the great man, promised it never should, if she could help it.

Their first step was to despatch an invitation carefully framed to Mount-Maurice Castle, begging that Lord and Lady Mount-Maurice would accept the hospitality of their affectionate relatives during the coming month; and though the old nobleman must have seen through the policy that dictated the letter, he graciously accepted the invitation, too glad, no doubt, to save himself the rent of a furnished house during an expensive season. It only now remained to fit up suitable apartments, and Mrs. Ainslie at once cast her eyes on the day and night nurseries, to which the poor dead mother had devoted two of the finest bedrooms in the house. As Mr. Ainslie had never been an over-affectionate father, it was not difficult to persuade him that a residence of some months in the country would be highly beneficial to the children; and they were accordingly despatched with Nana to the cottage of one of her friends in Devonshire. The air was beautiful, the scenery lovely, and the house surrounded by fields and gardens; but the greatest charm of their new abode, in Nurse Murphy's eyes, was the fact that it was next door to a Catholic church, and that the priest of that church was Father Bernard, her dear dead mistress's old and only friend.

They started, and, the field once clear, Mrs. Anslie spared neither money nor pains in the decoration of the apartments for the use of the expected guests, who arrived just when all was completed. At the first meeting at which Lord Mount-Maurice was to be one of the speakers, Mrs. Ainslie was present among his friends upon the platform. Little fear had she of being recognised by any of her old Catholic companions, had it been possible for any to be present; she well knew how little similarity there was between the elegantly dressed Mrs. Ainslie and the Louisa Trevor of old, with her poke-bonnet and long cloak, and favourite market-basket.

As the days rolled by, Lord and Lady Mount-Maurice grew more and more enchanted with their new kinswoman, whose orthodoxy they never for an instant questioned, until the chance remark of a caller revealed the awful fact that the new Mrs. Ainslie, like the first one, was a Papist. They were of course terribly shocked at first, and even angry; but she spoke so sweetly and gushingly of her struggles after truth, begged so prettily for their prayers to enable her to find it, and received so gratefully the homilies and tracts of the old nobleman, that he was quite propitiated, and talked of her already as of a brand half snatched from the burning.

The visit came to an end that very week, and Lord and Lady Mount-Maurice returned to the country, expressing themselves more than delighted with their visit, and giving their hospitable relations a cordial invitation for the ensuing autumn. It was of course in due time accepted; and while Mr. Ainslie joined other kindred spirits in shooting hares and partridges, his wife sat at home with the old couple, either retailing her own experiences, till Lord Mount-Maurice's white head shook like a mandarin's, or else listening to his harangues till her own ached. The result of these conferences was at last revealed in a paragraph that went the round of all the 'Low Church' papers:

'Among the guests at present assembled at Mount-Maurice Castle, the seat of Lord Grosvenor Mount-Maurice,—so well known to the world by his labours in the cause of the Gospel —are Mr. and Mrs. Ainslie, of Mulgrave-square.

We have it on good authority that this highly gifted lady, after vainly seeking peace in the errors of Ritualism and Romanism, has once more returned to the Church of her fathers. We beg to congratulate her.'

The new spare rooms were found so very convenient by Mrs. Ainslie, and such good accounts reached home of the health and happiness of the children, that the weeks appointed for their stay in Devonshire grew into months, and these into a term of two years. Indeed, it was not until Nana's services were in requisition for Mrs. Ainslie's own infant daughter that the order for their return was issued.

The letter arrived on the morning of Hubert's tenth birthday. There was of course a pleasurable excitement about the journey, and a little wish on the children's part to see dear papa and new mamma, and the still newer baby; nevertheless, that letter was a disappointment even to the children, and a bitter, bitter trial to poor old Nana. But to hear was to obey, and she wrote off by return of post to announce to her master and mistress that she would give up the rooms and make all arrangements for their journey as speedily as possible.

Everything was of course hurry-skurry at once. No morning walk as usual, no nice quiet dinner, but packing, packing everywhere, and a hurried meal, snatched almost as quickly and uncomfortably as though they were already dining at a railway station. For one thing, however, Nana found due and proper leisure, and we rather imagine that it was for that she had put on steam so vigorously all the morning. In honour of Hubert's birthday all three were to take tea with Father Bernard; and just as the clock struck four they presented themselves in his parlour, the children washed, combed, and tidivated to the highest pitch of perfection, and Nana herself looking as cool and collected as though there were no such things as packing and journeys, and sorrowful partings and fickle new mistresses, in the world.

Neither Father Bernard nor Nana had read that paragraph in the papers; but they both knew well that the children were going to a silly feather-headed woman, with whom religion was as much a whim as any other of her ephemeral hobbies. While the children laughed and frolicked and 'kept shop' on the broad window-sill, the priest and the old nurse sat and talked over so many sad possibilities and probabilities that, had it not been for their confidence in God, their very hearts would have fainted within them.

They cheered up and had a very nice evening for all that, for both of them loved the little ones too well to cloud with sad forebodings the happiness of the birthday treat. So while they ate bread-and-butter, strawberries and cream, and a host of other niceties, Father Bernard told them funny stories of his schoolboy days, and afterwards had such a game with them in the garden at hide and seek, that Nana and the housekeeper, who watched them from the door, could hardly fancy Father Bernard was not a child himself, instead of a hoary old gentleman of nearly eighty summers.

But when all was over, and the children came to bid him good-night and receive his parting blessing, he laid a hand on each little head, and looked into their eyes with an expression one, at least, never forgot. 'Children, you are going away from me to-morrow, and, in all human probability, I shall never see you more. For, at eighty years of age, it is nearly bed-time—yes, bed-time, children—for the weary body, though a glad awakening, let us hope and pray, for the ransomed soul to God. Hubert, you are now ten years of age. Will you promise Father Bernard, your own old father, and your mother's and grandmother's early friend, one thing?'

'Yes, father,' said the boy.

'Promise me, then, that nothing shall ever make you false to your faith. Children young as you have been martyrs before now; and you have only to pray as they did, and God will make you firm as He made them. You may never be tried; I pray, indeed, with all my heart and soul that you never may ; but, in case the hour of trial should come, kneel down this moment and promise God that neither promises, threats, punishments, nor even death itself shall separate you from Him and His Holy Church, into which you have been baptised. Will you promise this?' he asked, bending his piercing eyes upon him.

'Yes, father,' said the child, falling on his knees, and looking thoroughly awestruck.

' Then good-night, my boy—good-night, dear children, and God bless you ; and remember, Hubert, He will bless and prosper you as you keep that promise.'

It was the last time they ever saw Father Bernard. He was saying Mass next morning when the farmer drove them to the early train ; and, before the spring flowers bloomed next year, the old priest had fallen into the sleep of which he had told them.

Hubert's constancy was to be put to the proof much sooner than his friends had imagined, for on the morning of the first day at home the storm broke. Lord and Lady Mount-Maurice, who were up in town for a few days, were again Mrs. Ainslie's guests, and, partly to exhibit herself in the amiable light of a loving stepmother, partly to show off little Emmeline's beauty and vivacity, that lady issued orders that the children should take their dinner when she and her guests lunched.

All were seated in solemn silence at table, waiting for the covers to be removed by the stately butler.

'Let us ask a blessing,' said his lordship, reverently joining his hands, and casting down his eyes.

Those of her ladyship, however, chanced to be raised, and, to her horror, she saw, as plainly as eyes could see, Hubert and his sister make a large sign of the Cross.

'What!' she exclaimed as soon as grace was ended. 'Surely, my dear Louisa, you are not going to allow these sweet children to be brought up Papists?'

'Certainly not, my dear Lady Mount-Maurice; certainly not! Hubert and Emmeline, do you hear, you are not to do that again! They only returned home from the country late last night, and I have not yet taken them in hand,' she explained, turning her eyes sweetly to each noble guest in turn. 'But I will soon put everything to rights now I have them at home. Their mother, you know, poor dear,' she added aside, in an apologising tone, 'was a Romanist. No worse than some one else, you will say,' she continued, assuming a pretty air of self-condemnation; 'and, indeed, I only wish I could plead her excuse for my past folly, for she, poor thing, was born in error. But these sweet darlings must be trained to better things. I promise you they shall not be Roman Catholics long.'

'Yes, I will,' broke in Hubert fearlessly. 'I will be a Catholic till I die. If you crucified me like the little Japanese boy, or fried me like St. Lawrence, or tore me up into little tiny pieces, I would still be a Catholic—so there!'

'And tho will I!' lisped a little voice beside him.

'Of course you will, Emmy. Our own dear mamma was a Catholic, and we won't be nasty old Protestants for anybody!'

Of course both culprits were ordered from the table instanter, and of course they immediately made their way to Nana, who comforted and petted the now sobbing Hubert in every way she could devise. Her open declaration that the dear child was right, and her evident determination to aid and abet him in his rebellion, would have been followed by Nana's instant dismissal; but then, as Mrs. Ainslie argued, what could she have done with dear baby? But, although Nana could not be removed from her darlings, to her bitter sorrow they were removed from her. Lady Mount-Maurice, who had lost a favourite granddaughter about Emmeline's age, took such a fancy to the bright-haired little girl that, for the remainder of her visit, she would hardly allow her to leave her side. She at length summoned courage to offer to adopt her, and, somewhat to her astonishment, not only the stepmother, but even Mr. Ainslie himself, consented with hardly any demur. When her ladyship returned to the country Emmeline accompanied her, never again to take her place in her father's heart or home, but resigned, body and soul, for policy's sake, to her new protectress.

The day after her departure poor Hubert was placed in the establishment of a certain Dr. Parkins. There, in addition to the usual war waged on little boys, the child found himself constantly compelled to fight single-handed an individual one of his own. But he came off victorious in the end. For, though it was an easy matter to prevent a child of ten hearing Mass or frequenting the Sacraments, nothing but brute force could have compelled him to eat meat on days of abstinence, to attend the Protestant services or school prayers, or even to learn a single line of the 'Church Catechism ;' and this, fortunately, Dr. Parkins was far too much of a gentleman to employ, notwithstanding Mrs. Ainslie's stringent orders. Indeed, it soon became apparent that both he and all the masters secretly loved and admired the little child, who thus boldly defied them all for conscience' sake, although his meekness and obedience in other things made him a pattern to the whole school. Hubert Ainslie was also a general favourite with the boys, and it was by their connivance that he occasionally broke bounds to pay a visit to a certain little church, which brief stolen visits amply repaid him for many a wretched hour. Night and morning, too, he said the prayers Nana had taught him, and thus, in spite of all that could be done, said, or threatened, remained as firm a little Catholic as even the old priest or the old nurse could have desired to see him.

He was never, except for a day or two at Christmas, sent home for the holidays, but invariably passed them at the seaside under the charge of a master, in company with a few youths from the Colonies, and Nana, finding all hopes of protecting her darlings at an end, relinquished Mrs. Ainslie's service as soon as those hopes had fled. She, however, remained in London, and was permitted by Dr. Parkins to pay an occasional visit to her boy, who generally nestled in her arms close to her large warm heart all the time the visit lasted, as though it were the only refuge left him upon earth.

Things remained thus till Hubert was fourteen, and had earned for himself the reputation of the cleverest boy in the school. But the over-study that had developed his brain had also stunted his growth and impaired his health;

and, about this time, he was seized with a sudden and very serious illness.

Mr. and Mrs. Ainslie were, of course, summoned at once, but the latter, who had lately developed a whim for invalidism, declared that a sick-room would be far too much for her nerves. The father, therefore, went alone, and, really touched by the pinched and mournful expression of the young face, for the first time in his life perhaps, felt a real interest in and affection for his boy. The fact that his son's life was in actual danger never seemed to enter his mind, until the old doctor shook his head in answer to his now anxious questioning, and then the poor man felt precisely as any other parent would feel in similar circumstances. Physicians were summoned without regard to expense, and so eager was he that anything and everything should be done that could either benefit or please the child, that when Hubert timidly asked him to grant him a favour he did so at once, without even asking what it was; and when he found it was only that he might be allowed to see a priest, he hurried off there and then, and fetched one himself.

But Hubert did not die. The disease took a turn from the day of that first confession and first Communion, both made within an hour of Mr. Ainslie granting his son's request. Nana was sent to tend him, and after a month's nursing from her at school, and another month's petting down at the dear old place in Devonshire, Hubert was himself again. He spent a week or two at home before returning to school, and Mr. Ainslie, much of whose tenderness had vanished with the boy's restored health and strength, tried more than once to coerce him into conformity with the State Church. But in vain; if Hubert had been strong before, he was lion-like now in the strength of the Bread of Life, and his father once again relinquished the attempt as hopeless.

One long yearning wish of the boy's heart was satisfied by this visit home, but, alas! in a most unsatisfactory manner. He had never seen his sister Emmeline since her adoption by Lady Mount-Maurice, and when, on arriving in London, he was told that she also was at home on a brief visit, his delight knew no bounds. But the Emmeline he found was a very different little personage from the Emmeline of his loving dreams, and though she was even more beautiful, and greeted him with a long fond kiss at first, it soon became apparent to him that Mount-Maurice Castle was now her home, and the spot where all her affections centred. She talked of nothing and no one but Lady Mount-Maurice and Cecil the young orphan heir, who shared with her the old lady's love and solicitude. As to any word on the subject next

his heart, it was out of the question. Hubert
soon found it as difficult to approach it with
her as it might have been with Lady Mount-
Maurice. Nana she had no wish to see; Father
Bernard she had quite forgotten; and when he
spoke in his own impassioned manner of their
mother's faith, and showed her their mother's
prayer-book, the girl of twelve only honoured
the one with a pious little sigh of compassion,
and laid down the other with a shake of the
head worthy of the old lord himself. Crushed in
his tenderest affection Hubert returned to school,
never again to associate Emmeline with one
happy or holy thought. A halo of sisterly love
still, however, hovered around him, cheering
many a lonely minute, but it was the love of
Ethel, his little half-sister, now four years of age,
who, during his brief visit home, had devoted
herself to him heart and soul, the proudest
little maiden possible in the possession of a
big brother.

Not very big either; for he was a stunted,
slender, ugly boy; and when, a few years later,
he entered at Oxford, he was a diminutive and
still uglier man. Possibly this unprepossess-
ing exterior, combined with his retiring habits,
shielded him from many a temptation. For
although amply supplied with means, he fre-
quented no amusements, entertained no company, made few friends. His whole time was

given to study; and having passed several brilliant examinations, and taken a good degree, he returned to London, and for the first time since his early childhood took up his residence at home.

And a very miserable home he found it, in spite of his ever-increasing affection for his sister Ethel, now a bright sunny girl of twelve. For not only had Mrs. Ainslie's love of pleasure degenerated into reckless extravagance and utter neglect of her duties, but her whimsical exacting temper embittered almost every hour of every day. What to Hubert were his costly surroundings, what the obsequious attentions of the servants, if it all had to be enjoyed in an atmosphere of perpetual discord? What to him was the stalled ox, if it had to be eaten with bitter herbs, in the form of sarcastic innuendoes perpetually hurled against the faith by that apostate tongue?

Yet, hard as all this was to bear, it was not Hubert's greatest trial. The cross that pressed most heavily on the young man's heart was a strange and inexplicable change that had latterly come over his father. It seemed almost impossible to recognise the once free-hearted Robert Ainslie in the silent morose being who would now sometimes sit silent for hours, bowed as though half the troubles of the world rested on his shoulders, communing, apparently, with the blackest and bitterest thoughts. That the restored health of the young heir of Mount-Maurice had put an end to his father's dreams concerning his succession to the title and estates, Hubert knew well. But he knew also that it must have been something more than such a disappointment to change the whole tenor of his life and blanch his hair, as Robert Ainslie's was blanching now. Did the cause lie in the frightful extravagance of Mrs. Ainslie's household expenditure, or was it to be sought in something else, the secret of which only Mr. Ainslie knew?

Over and above these various subjects of anxiety, moreover, Hubert had one peculiarly his own in the question of his future career. Not a word on the subject had ever been mooted by either his father or Mrs. Ainslie; and, at the age of twenty-three, not only did he crave for the independence due to his age and education, but was looking forward ardently to a future long the subject of his dreams. Even from his boyhood, the Bar had been the object of Hubert's highest ambition, and the lives of eminent barristers his favourite reading. Debarred by the circumstances of his education from Catholic surroundings, society, and literature, the innate love of God and zeal for His glory, that would probably have developed early into a vocation for the priesthood, had turned to this profession as embodying to him all that was highest, holiest, most godlike upon earth. With a devotion nothing short of the enthusiasm of a young knight-errant, he too looked forward to the hour when he should stand forth to overthrow the oppressor, avenge the innocent, and uphold the cause of God and truth in an unjust iniquitous age. And as a young esquire may have fought doughty battles in perspective, and waved in fancy the good sword with which he was not yet girded, so did Hubert Ainslie, by his bedroom fire, rehearse the passionate pleading that was one day to make sordid counsellors hide their diminished heads, to melt the jurymen and the very judge himself, and to let all who should hear him understand what meant the majesty of the law.

That his father would propose to take him into his own office, and strongly resent his choice of another calling, was his daily fear; and morning after morning and evening after evening he sat awaiting the mandate to take his seat at the desk. When weeks had lengthened into a month, and that again into two, it suddenly struck him that his father must be waiting for him to speak first on the subject; and although, in Mr. Ainslie's altered mood, he felt as if he would as soon have bearded a lion, he called up all the courage he possessed, and resolved to address him on the subject.

He chose as his opportunity the moment when Mrs. Ainslie and Ethel had retired, and left his father and himself alone in the dining-room. The voice of the young man almost failed as he broached the subject; but he warmed as he proceeded to paint, in his own energetic way, all he hoped to compass with his father's consent and coöperation. He paused at length for an answer; it came in the form of a bitter sarcastic laugh, followed by such a storm of invective against his evil fortune, against his wife, against even Providence, that Hubert fairly shuddered. Gradually Mr. Ainslie recovered himself, and the paroxysm subsided; but it was only to tell his son never again to look to him for help, since ruin, utter hopeless ruin, and that at no distant day, stared him in the face. As his father spoke slowly and hissingly, the whole fabric of Hubert's hopes crumbled to the ground, never to rise again. For a moment he sat staring at the wreck, but it was only for a moment. The next his conscience had bitterly reproached him for his selfishness, and not one other thought did Hubert Ainslie that night bestow on the broken dream of his life.

They sat late into the night, over a heap of books and papers, Mr. Ainslie trying to explain and Hubert straining every nerve to understand the miserable complication that lay before them. Only once were they disturbed, when Mrs. Ainslie, outraged by their suffering the coffee to grow cold, marched suddenly in to demand the reason of their neglect. The question was never asked; for the faces that met her angry glance were so wan and white as they looked up at her almost mechanically, that for once in her life Louisa Ainslie felt thoroughly cowed. When the man-servant entered the drawing-room late at night, thinking all had retired, he was startled at her terrified expression as she turned her face upon him.

'She looked,' he said afterwards in the servants' hall, ' for all the world as if she had seen a ghost,' and certainly if any woman ever saw a banshee or bodha-glas, Louisa Ainslie had seen one that night in her husband's eyes.

No conclusion could be arrived at concerning Mr. Ainslie's affairs ; but it was easy to come to a very decided one concerning Hubert's. He, at least, must find something to do at once.

'For your own sake,' said the father.

'For everybody's,' thought poor Hubert, positively shivering at the idea of remaining another day in dependence on his already overburdened parent.

The very next morning, in compliance with a suggestion from his father, Hubert set off for Mount-Maurice Castle, praying earnestly that the old nobleman might be induced to employ in his behalf the patronage he was known to possess. It was a journey of many hours, and it was already dusk when he arrived, an unexpected guest. He was civilly, though not very warmly, received. Even Emmeline, whose heart had evidently drifted farther away from him than ever, after the first cold kiss and a few chilling inquiries about her parents, had seemed almost at a loss for a subject of conversation, and, *faute de mieux*, had given the weather a very decided prominence in her remarks. But the entrance of the young heir with the result of his day's shooting at once brought the light to her eyes and life to her manner, and Hubert saw plainly that, if his sister had been bound to Mount-Maurice before by ties of filial and sisterly affection, those ties were now strengthened by a bond still stronger, never to be broken save by the hand of death itself. He saw, too, and saw truly that night, that, as the future Lady Mount-Maurice, Emmeline Ainslie would be separated for ever from the Church of her baptism.

He had plenty of time to think of all these things, for, directly dinner was over, a carriage drove round to take the whole party to a meeting concerning the 'spread of the Gospel in Italy,' at which Lord Mount-Maurice had promised to take the chair. They gave Hubert an invitation to accompany them, which he politely refused, greatly to their disgust, and was left to spend the evening as best he might, *solus cum solo*, amongst a very doleful set of old books, in the library.

'And so your father wants me to give you a lift in the world, does he?' asked Lord Mount-Maurice, as he and his visitor sat *tête-à-tête* next morning in his lordship's private room. 'Well, well, tell me all about it;' and the old gentleman displayed a whole set of false teeth in a smile so benevolent that the heart of the young one beat high with expectation. He told Lord Mount-Maurice as much as he judged expedient of his father's embarrassments, and concluded by telling him how grateful they would both be if he could help him to the start he so much needed.

'I hear you have done well at Oxford.'

Hubert briefly and modestly sketched his University career.

'Good. Well, sir, I may as well tell you at once that my brother-in-law, who, as you are probably aware, is a man of considerable interest with the present Government, told me only the other day that he knew of a capital post for just such a young fellow as yourself. The salary commences at 500*l.* per annum, but to a man of *savoir-faire*, it would not stand long at that. Now I believe, from what I hear and know, that you are in many ways eminently qualified for this post; yes, sir, eminently qualified,' he repeated, in answer to the sudden brightening of the young man's eyes; '*but*,' and the emphasis on the disjunctive was so emphatic that the brightness fled instanter, 'there is a proviso, sir, and a very strong one, too.'

If ever a look was 'intense,' it was that of Hubert at this moment.

'You are, I believe, sir, a Roman Catholic?'

'Yes, my lord, I am; but our religion has ceased to be a disqualification for holding positions under Government. Catholics now occupy the very highest offices.'

'Yes, to our shame and cost they do; but woe to the Government that allows it! Our Government, sir, does not do its duty to the religion of the State; and depend upon it, this unhappy country, sooner or later, will suffer for the blindness of its rulers. But I intend, at any rate, to do my duty; and never will I propose for any office whatsoever a single man who does not hold the soundest Protestant principles. Were I to recommend a Romanist for such a post as this—a post where a man of talent might rise to almost any eminence in the Government of the country—I should consider myself every whit as guilty as though I had lighted a match to kindle another fire in Smithfield. So now, sir, it remains for you to choose: renounce, as our Emmeline has done, the errors and superstitions of Rome; embrace the Gospel of Christ, as she has embraced it, and I promise, on the word of a Christian nobleman, to befriend you as warmly, as truly, ay, and as tenderly, as I have befriended her. She is, I may tell you, about to be openly affianced to our grandson; and you will believe me when I say that I am quite prepared to acknowledge that, after Cecil and herself, no one shall have as near a claim on me as our darling Emmeline's brother. But you must be a Protestant, man; you must be a Protestant. There, go and consider what I have said. I give you the day to decide in.'

A day? In less than a minute, a firm, bold, but respectful confession of the Faith, unchanged and unchangeable, had scattered Lord Mount-Maurice's patronage, and Hubert's new-born hopes, to the winds. Half an hour later, after formal adieux to the whole family, Emmeline included—Emmeline's, perhaps, from her anger and annoyance, the most formal adieu of all—Hubert had taken leave of Mount-Maurice Castle, and once again found himself whirling on as fast as steam could carry him.

Not, however, direct to London; for having remembered that Nana's present residence lay on his way home, he determined to stop and gladden her dear old heart by spending the night at her cottage. Her delight at the unexpected appearance of her boy, whom she had not seen for years, and hardly hoped to see again, may be better imagined than described. Nor was Hubert's attention to his old nurse unrewarded; for her hearty applause of his conduct, and her loving words of trust in God, fell like balm upon his wounded spirit, and nerved him, as perhaps nothing else could have done, for the dreaded task that lay before him of detailing his ill-success to his father.

An unfortunate circumstance, however, that Hubert had not foreseen, resulted from his visit to Nana, since it gave Emmeline time to write to her father a long and bitterly worded account of her brother's interview with Lord Mount-Maurice. Hardly had he dismissed the cab and put down his portmanteau than a little figure flew across the hall and nestled sobbing in his arms.

'O Hubert, Hubert! what have you done to make papa so very angry with you?'

'Angry, darling? I have not seen him for two days.'

'Yes; but he has had a letter from Mount-Maurice Castle. He has not shown it to mamma, but she says he is in a terrible rage with you. O Hubert! I am so frightened.'

'Silly child! I will go and talk to him, and it will soon come all right, as you will see.'

But Hubert's face as he knocked at the door of his father's room sadly belied his statement; and it was not exactly in the tones of a man who has nothing to fear that he wished his father good-evening when he entered.

'It's you, sir, is it?' said Mr. Ainslie, who was

seated at his writing-desk, in the full glare of a lamp, with an open letter beside him. 'Bad evening, I should rather say, and bad everything else where you are concerned, bad luck included. Well, sir! a pretty mess you have made of it at Mount-Maurice.'

'Indeed, father, it was not my fault. I am sorry to say—'

'Not your fault, indeed!' growled Mr. Ainslie, 'and you're sorry to say! So am I sorry to have to own such a fool for my son! Why, sir, your fortune was positively as much in your own hands as this ruler is in mine. In your own hands, sir! do you hear? and here you have gone and missed it all for a parcel of humbug and tomfoolery that went out of fashion three hundred years ago. I am ashamed of you, that I am! I declare a cat or dog would have served its own interests better.'

'But, father, my conscience—'

'Your conscience!' repeated Mr. Ainslie, with a stinging emphasis on the word. 'Let us have bread-and-cheese first, and conscience after, if you please, my good fellow. Besides, consciences like yours are far too fine for everyday wear and tear. At any rate, they won't do for me, so you must just please to make your own way in the world. I am not rich enough to set up a private lunatic asylum, so you had better start off and find somebody who can. I have worse than beggared myself for the sake of my wife and her whims, and I have no notion of sacrificing, ay, criminating myself—let the word out if it will—still further for the sake of my son and his conscience.'

'Do you really wish me to go, father?'

'Of course I do.'

'At once?'

'At once, this very night; what earthly use are you to me, I should like to know?'

'Let us at least part kindly, father.'

'The greatest kindness you can show me is never to let me see your face again. Don't bother me any more. I have more than enough to send me mad already, without prating to you. Good-night.'

Like one in a dream, Hubert walked out of the room, and, closing the door behind him, stood still on the softly-carpeted hall, looking round for his little sister. She was not there; but through the half-open door of a small boudoir he could see her sitting by the fire, crooning a low mournful air to herself, as she stroked the silken fringes of a little dog that lay on her lap. He had crossed the hall, and had almost reached the door, when the rustle of his stepmother's dress, descending the stairs, caught his ear. Swiftly and noiselessly he turned away, and, taking up his hat, great-coat, and portmanteau, that still stood on the chair, passed out into the night.

He knew not, cared not, whither; but for two long hours sped rapidly on, clearing mile after mile of London streets, and only pausing when he found his progress checked by the door of a stable, which suddenly terminated a street he had been traversing. As he turned to retrace his steps a feeling of dizziness and weariness crept over him, and reminded him that he had tasted no food since breakfast, except a few biscuits that Nana had slipped into his pocket just as he was starting for the station. After resting himself for a few minutes, by leaning against a wall, Hubert once more took up his valise and continued his journey. But reaction had followed the intense excitement that had hitherto sustained him, and, though he still continued his course, such utter weariness and faintness had supervened that he almost tottered as he walked.

He had reached a somewhat quiet suburb, and few and far between were the pedestrians he now encountered on the road. So few indeed did these become as the evening advanced that he stood still, waiting in vain for some kindly passer-by who might inform him into what part of the world he had wandered.

He was standing in front of a pair of iron gates, behind which the outline of a Gothic building reared itself high into the dreary darkness; and never in the whole of his lonely life had he felt so utterly alone, so utterly forsaken. Suddenly the sound of an organ pealed out in the church behind him, and, to his intense delight, he recognised the glorious and familiar accents of the 'O Salutaris Hostia,' Hunger, weariness, loneliness, all were forgotten, as he drank in the welcome notes; and before another minute had elapsed, Hubert was kneeling, one of a large crowd of adoring worshippers. That tears of emotion stood in his eyes we may well believe, as he found himself thus suddenly brought into that glorious Presence, of which he as yet knew so little, but for which he had unhesitatingly sacrificed so much.

As soon as Benediction was over, Hubert made his way to the sacristy, and inquired of a priest he found there if he could tell him of a lodging where he could remain for the night. There was something in the voice and manner of the young man that at once attracted the attention of the good religious, and, with a few kindly questions, he soon succeeded in drawing from him a brief history of his misfortunes. Not that it was told then. Father Felix needed few words to tell him that Hubert was sadly in need of food and rest, and it was before a cheerful fire in the 'visitors' room,' and over an ample supper, that the story was poured into the sympathetic ear of his new friend. Great was Hubert's delight on learning that Father Felix had not only known Father Bernard, but that it was to him he attributed his conversion and his vocation, and all the grace and happiness that had accrued to him from both.

Neither that night, nor for several days after, did Hubert Ainslie leave that hospitable roof, where each holy inmate, down to the old lay-brother at the gate, seemed to vie with each other in heaping kindnesses upon him. When at length he turned his steps from the door it was only to take possession of a comfortable lodging in an adjoining street, and with the prospect of a cosy little salary to be derived from a clerkship the good father had obtained for him.

The morning after his arrival at the monastery, Hubert had written to his father a letter couched in terms of the deepest respect and affection, expressing his regret at the disappointment he had been compelled to cause him, and assuring him that he would do all in his power to turn to advantage the education he had given him. As he feared to give the address of his present home, he gave that of a neighbouring post-office, but though he trudged to the place several times a day no answer awaited him. A second letter brought the same result, and Hubert then wrote to Ethel, begging her to do her utmost to soften their father's anger in his regard. He put to this the address of his new apartments, and the first letter handed to him after his arrival was his own to his sister, returned to him in his stepmother's handwriting, without a single word of comment.

He had only been a fortnight in his new occupation, and had just resolved that he would pay a visit to his father and see what could be done by a personal interview, when a whisper began suddenly to circulate among the clerks that strange revelations were about to come to light concerning the secretary of a large City company. By the afternoon the name had transpired, and the rumour that said Robert Ainslie was the man told his son, as well as the other clerks, that he had fled the country, with his wife and daughter, to evade the arm of the law.

The instant Hubert could get away from the office he flew rather than walked to the old house, but it was only to find everything in the hands of the creditors. Nothing more than he had already heard could be obtained from the person in charge, and without even expressing a wish to enter the house, Hubert turned away, sick at heart, to pour his grief into the sympathising ears of his new friends. They alone knew Hubert's secret. None of his fellow-clerks guessed for a moment that there was any connection between the quiet Ainslie, their new clerk, and the Ainslie whose defalcation was the theme of every tongue throughout the City.

Time sped on his road till two years had passed away; and, though the wound of many a fiery trial still remained, Hubert Ainslie's soul had found a peace and calm to which he had been a stranger in the past. 'Every soul knoweth its own bitterness,' and only those who really knew him understood the shadow that often stole over his face, even in his calmest moments. It was not an easy thing for an upright honest heart, loving God and man, to think of a father fugitive from his native land for having broken its laws. Nor was it less grievous for a loving brother and fervent Catholic to see the name of the young Lord and Lady Mount-Maurice paraded in the newspaper paragraphs, that described the funeral of the late nobleman, as patronising the Irish Church Missions, and entertaining a noted arch-apostate and his wife at Mount-Maurice.

Possessing more than enough for his own requirements, Hubert made no attempt to improve his position, but plodded quietly on, content with his lot. Perhaps his contentment may have had something to do with a secret that had never yet been breathed to mortal ear, but which more than one of the fathers read in that pale young face, as Hubert remained for hours together absorbed in devotion before the altar.

It was a dark tempestuous night, and a wild equinoctial gale was roaring down the chimneys and round the house-tops, and driving the rain in torrents against the windows. Hubert, who had been kept unusually late at the office, had just finished his dinner, and was enjoying a quiet half-hour with a book. A grand mission had been going on at the church for the last fortnight, so well attended that one might have imagined the world stood at last a very fair chance of being converted, and Hubert, to whom a mission was quite a new experience, had hardly missed a sermon. But, though he quite meant to go to the evening sermon, he had, he found, still half an hour's grace, and so the young man put his feet on the fender and became very soon absorbed in his book.

He was interrupted by a tap at the door, and the landlady, entering, informed him that a person who had already called twice that evening was below, and asking to see him.

'A tall middle-aged lady,' was Mrs. Madden's description.

'A lady! I know no ladies, Mrs. Madden.'

'This one knows you, howsomedever, sir; and she's a lady for all as she has hardly a decent rag to her back. From the look of her I should say she's just over an illness. "It's a bad night for such as you to be out on, ma'am," says I, but never a word did she answer. I should have told you about her before, Mr. Ainslie, for she said as how she'd call again; but I was out when you come in.'

'You can ask her to walk up, though I expect it is some mistake,' said Hubert; 'I know nobody of that description.'

He was right; he had never known any one like the woman who presented herself, battered by the wind and drenched by the rain, crushed moreover by poverty, and emaciated by want. But he had known another woman whose pride and wickedness had blighted his life. Somehow or other these two women, in one overwhelming duality, stood before him with downcast eyes. He was no believer in phantoms, and yet it was so difficult to realise that Louisa Ainslie stood there in the flesh, that it was not until she actually spoke that he felt quite certain she was not a spectre, or a creature of his own imagination.

'Hubert,' she said softly, and there was so much deep suffering in her voice that it thrilled him through and through—'Hubert, your father is, I fear, dying, and I have come to fetch you to him.'

'Dying? where? not in London?'

'Yes, in London; not very far from here.'

'Dying, and here!' he repeated, as though stupefied; 'I heard you were all abroad.'

'It was only a blind to escape from the

creditors. We have never left London, but have gone from hiding-place to hiding-place, lower and lower each time, till now we are in a very den of misery.'

'And where is Ethel?'

'In service.'

Even the gentle nature of Hubert Ainslie exploded in a wrathful exclamation.

'What else could I do for a child of her age, Hubert? It was that or slow starvation, and there is no real disgrace in it, after all.'

'No,' said the young man, as the words, 'He took upon Him the form of a servant,' seemed to flash in letters of light before his eyes; 'but why have I never known all this before?'

'Because—I will tell you the real truth, Hubert —because, until a few days, a very few days ago, this heart'—and she struck her breast wildly as she spoke—'this heart was the abode of devils; yes, of devils as black as any of the seven that ravaged the soul of Mary Magdalene. You could hardly have left the house before your poor father, whose temper was never worse than a flash in the pan, came to inquire for you. In his grief and terrror at finding that you had taken him at his word, he broke into a terrible passion; and I, instead of soothing him, added fuel to the fire, as God knows I have often done, before and since, during my married life. The result was a fearful quarrel, in which he heaped a few false as well as many true accusations against me. The former were all I heard, and I longed to be revenged on him, and when your letter was handed to me next morning I at once flung it into the fire. Calm reflection showed me the folly, as well as the wickedness, of the act, but although I refrained from destroying the next, I locked it carefully up. In the same way I kept the address of your letter to Ethel before returning it, which I did unknown to any one. Many a time since our misfortunes began, even for my own sake, I have longed to summon you. I knew you could and would have helped us. But my crime brought its own punishment, for I positively feared to tell your father what I had done, even if my pride would have allowed me to humble myself to the confession.'

She paused, but Hubert only looked inquiringly, as though waiting for the rest.

'It was one day last week,' continued Mrs. Ainslie, 'that we removed into this neighbourhood, and one evening, in utter desperation, I started up here with a half hope I might chance to meet you, and tell you of our wretched condition. I had no single thought but relief in our terrible misery; and when I reached the church of which your letter spoke, and saw the door open, I turned in with no other hope but that of finding you, and obtaining from you bread for the next day. Whether or not you were present in that densely crowded mass I cannot say. I saw nothing but the preacher, I heard nothing but his words on mortal sin. Hubert, God's grace alone had carried me to that church. I have been there every night since. He has forgiven me the black ingratitude of the last twelve years. Last night I went to confession. This morning He came to me Himself as a pledge of pardon. If He has forgiven me, will not you forgive me too, dear boy ?'

The convulsive sob with which he pressed her attenuated form to his heart was his only answer.

Good Mrs. Madden was very much astonished when she was called up and asked if she had another room to spare in her house. When she said the large front bedroom was to let, she was still more astonished; for Hubert took it then and there, and told her to light a rousing fire in it at once, and to order in port-wine, calf's-foot jelly, chops, and everything else proper for an invalid.

An hour later Hubert was sitting by the most wretched bed he had ever imagined, in the most forlorn of garrets, holding his father's poor wasted hand in his. All the night long he sat there whispering so much affection, and talking of so many bright things in the future, that quite a hopeful twinkle shone once more in the sick man's weary eyes. The very next afternoon Mr. Ainslie was carefully wrapped in blankets and taken in a cab to Hubert's lodgings, where Mrs. Ainslie and Ethel already awaited them, the latter just as sweet and ladylike, despite her experience as a nursemaid, as when her brother had last seen her stroking Bijou's silken fringes.

Thanks to the tender care bestowed on him by Hubert and his repentant wife, Mr. Ainslie so far recovered as to live for nearly two years, though he never recovered his wonted health or strength. But he found in these last two years something incomparably better than either, inasmuch as the soul is higher than the body, and eternity of more account than time. Regret for his past folly, and contrition for his sins, were amongst the blessings and graces God gave him in the last two years of his life; and there was something even more than this. For one bright morning, at the same font, he and Ethel were baptised, and shortly afterwards, side by side, made their first Communion. When, a few months later, he passed away, it was in the arms of Hubert, and fortified by the Sacraments of the Church.

His death was a heavy blow to Hubert, who had begun to entertain hopes of his recovery; but he found consolation in the grateful solicitude of his stepmother, who never seemed as if she could sufficiently atone for the past. After her husband's death she would gladly have tried to earn her own livelihood, but Hubert would not hear of it. He sought and obtained a more lucrative appointment, and, having taken and furnished a small house, made a comfortable home for his mother and sister, where they have resided with him ever since.

Mrs. Ainslie has for years worked indefatigably in the parish of the priests who befriended her son; but though she is at the top and bottom, beginning and end, of nearly every good work in the place, it is rarely that a word passes her lips concerning her labours of love. To all but Hubert and Ethel she is shy and reserved, and mixes so little with the world that almost every minute not devoted to her work or her children is spent in earnest tearful prayer in the Church. God's will be done! In spite of all her prayers and all her tears, her stepdaughter still remains an alien to the faith of her fathers—an awful monument of the evils of a mixed marriage.

Had you asked me yesterday, or even this morning, I should have said that in all human probability the little household would cling together till divided by the hand of death. But I have heard strange news even to-day. About a month since, a maiden aunt of his mother's died, and bequeathed Hubert a sum of money so large that it enabled him to make restitution of nearly all his father had unjustly appropriated; and, over and above the sum required for that, he has settled a very comfortable competency on both Mrs. Ainslie and his sister. But I have heard even better news than this, from his own lips; for he and his old mother have been this very day to see me. I really cannot tell you who looked the happier of the two. God, my dear children, has crowned Hubert Ainslie's life of fidelity and sacrifice with the very greatest of earthly rewards. He starts for Rome to-morrow, to commence his studies for the priesthood, the happiest man alive, although—

'Although what, father?' asked Wild-Rose, for a pair of 'comical eyes' were fixed upon her blushing cheeks.

'Although he is a funny little man, with a big head, and a pair of eyes like the god what's-his-name's, a day's journey asunder.'

COUSIN PRUDENCE

The Tale of an Old Stocking.

CHAPTER I.

THE STOCKING ITSELF, AND HOW COUSIN PRUDENCE CAME BY IT.

I KNOW very well that it is not the custom for story-writers and story-tellers to go straight into the subject-matter of their stories at once. I do so, however, for fear my readers might imagine that I am about to commit the solecism of bringing into publicity certain small articles of my worthy cousin's attire generally kept out of view. I therefore hasten to premise that my story has nothing whatever to do with sundry little rolls, black, white, or gray, always so nattily folded and often so well darned, that used to lurk, and probably lurk still, in one corner of her top drawer. The stocking of which I am going to write, though it certainly belonged to cousin Prue, was a very different affair from any of these.

It was of coarse gray worsted, and big

enough, I should say, for Goliath of Gath. When it came into Prue's possession it was hanging at the head of the little bed that her mother had occupied ever since she could remember. The best thing about it at that epoch, in the eyes of most people, was its lining, which was composed of a good round number of pieces of gold and silver; for my worthy aunt Dorcas—God rest her soul!—had always been a thrifty woman, and though the sum (compared with many legacies) was not a large one, it was more than most women, possessing little more than a cottage and a small annuity of a few shillings a week, would have managed to lay by. It might have been even more if she could have placed it in the savings bank. But my aunt Dorcas eschewed banks of all kinds. Her husband had been ruined by one, and had broken his heart in consequence, just after Prudence's birth.

'It's a very fine place, no doubt,' she is said to have remarked upon seeing the Bank of England, 'a very fine place; but just give me my old stocking. Put your money into that, and there it is; put it into a place like that yonder, and where is it?'

The stocking was empty enough the week after it came into Prudence's possession. The neighbours told her that she ought to give her mother a grand funeral; that it would only be showing proper respect, &c.; and so the whole went in black velvet, nodding plumes, and a host of other lugubrious absurdities, the ostentation of which was terrible to poor meek, timid, little Prue; so terrible that, between worry and grief, it is almost a wonder that two coffins instead of one were not laid that time in the grave under the willow at the eastern corner of the Catholic churchyard.

The parish priest was so angry with Prudence for wasting her substance that he called (as he said afterwards) to give her a good scolding; but she received him so calmly and sweetly that he gave her his blessing instead. A great many people wondered why Father O'Connor talked so much just then about 'minding one's own business.' I think Prue and I made a pretty shrewd guess as to the reason.

Cousin Prue was soon her own dear little self again; for not only is Time a wonderful healer of sorrows, but from the very first hers had been of the kind the Divine Master promises shall be comforted. Within a short time after the funeral the little house was tidied up, each and every tiny room looking just the same as ever. But what a hard task that tidying up had been nobody ever knew; for cousin Prue, who had a wonderful knack of finding out other people's troubles, possessed another equally clever one of hiding her own. Not that she ever even tried to keep them from me. As only children of two sisters, both gone to a better world, Prue and I have always been all the world to one another, and never, I feel sure, has one had a secret that the other has not shared.

I was with her part of the time, and never shall I forget the turning out of my poor aunt's hoards, nor how strangely things, new and old, were jumbled together in her drawers and boxes. Reader, did it ever strike you or me, as we arrange our own particular little hoard, boasting, perhaps, that we can lay our hand on everything it contains, how strange a conglomeration it will present, when that hand shall be still for ever, to those who are destined to turn it over in our stead? How trivial objects will appear to them that some old association has perhaps enshrined in our very heart of hearts; how sacred, for some reminiscence connected with us, articles on which we ourselves may perhaps have set no value. Earthly, when all else points to heaven; material, when all else is of the spirit, to me the very saddest part of death is this disinterment of the daily life of the dead.

No; I shall never forget that day, nor how Prue's generosity triumphed even over her desire to retain her mother's things for herself. The only thing that enlivened the sadness of the task was the affectionate fights we had over almost everything good and pretty; though, to Prue's regret, I steadfastly refused them all, or nearly all. One thing, however, I did accept, and that was a coarse gray worsted stocking, evidently fellow to the one that had so long been aunt Dorcas's bank. With a real good laugh, the first we had had for many a day, I took possession of it, Prue and I agreeing that we would run a race, and see who would fill her stocking first with savings.

Notwithstanding our love and our cousinship, Prue's path and mine lay at that time in different directions; hers in the quiet seclusion of her native village, mine in the unquiet turmoil of my native London. Before that week was out my cousin and I, as well as the two old stockings, were more than a hundred miles asunder. As my story relates to Prue's stocking alone, I shall say no more just now of mine. Whether it was speedily filled to repletion with the coins of the realm, or remained long and lank as when I received it, matters nothing to my story. One thing, however, I may say *en passant.* If I did not save money, I could always justify myself on the plea that my old age was provided for. I certainly earned my living hardly enough at that time as a music-teacher; but my future gave me no uneasiness, since a moderate competency, now enjoyed by an octogenarian sister of my father's, was to revert to me at her death.

A year passed before I again saw cousin Prue, but at the end of that time I went to spend a much-needed holiday in the peaceful retreat of her dear little cottage. 'What a comfort it is to be going to her!' I said to myself, as the train bore me farther and farther away from the dust and din of the London streets, and the still worse din of the jingling of worn-out pianos in second and third rate schools. 'I wonder what her life is like, now poor aunt is no longer there to take up her time?' As we plunged deeper and deeper into a land of trees and meadows, I plunged deeper and deeper into my ruminations, which were only cut short by the train stopping at Handley station, and a well-known voice calling me by name.

For of course cousin Prue was on the platform to meet me, looking as sweet as ever in her well-kept mourning. In less than no time I was whirling along in the farmer's cart she had secured for my accommodation, every one we met in the little street smiling a welcome to me; for in Handley everybody knew everybody, and of course everybody's business too.

How the first evening of that visit to Prudence stands out above almost every other evening of my life! How delicious the milk and eggs and yellow creamy butter seemed, after the apologies for the same that I had been consuming in London! How different the very tea tasted, though I daresay in reality, having been bought at the little village shop, it was not even half as good as my own! And when, tea being finished and the tea-things washed up, we went out into the garden and sat side by side, under the canopy of the ivy-covered porch, how happy we both were!—Prue listening with glistening eyes and half-opened mouth to my stories of London life, and I drinking in the scent of the new-mown hay, the sleepy chirping of the birds, the droning of the bees, and all the other delicious country scents and sounds that came and went and floated around us in the soft evening air.

We had a very long talk next day about our respective ways and means, and I learned, to my surprise, that the clever little woman was already earning herself quite a reputation as a dressmaker among the villagers and farmers' wives around.

'And now, Prue,' said I, at the end of it, 'although you have been so fortunate, and made, I am sure, a great deal more money than you would spend in a year on your own modest wants, I feel morally certain you have never laid by a penny.'

Prue laughed most provokingly one of her very richest and merriest laughs.

'Ah, Prudence,' said I, shaking my head, as I had seen wise people do, 'it is all very well now, but remember sickness may come, and old age must, if you live long enough; and what will you do when you have no longer your fingers to fall back upon? Your income of ten pounds a year is not enough to keep body and soul together.'

Such a flash of mingled faith, hope, and charity shot across my cousin's face, that for a moment I felt almost awed; but I continued nevertheless,

'I never knew a person spend so little on herself as you do, Prue; I don't believe that ever in your life you bought a thing because it was pretty, or because you took a fancy to it, now did you?' I asked.

'I am sure I don't know,' said Prue, opening her eyes and trying to think; 'perhaps I find it more sensible to buy things that I really want.'

'Or rather that you cannot possibly do without,' I said half angrily: 'and yet, my dear cousin, notwithstanding all this self-denial, I have no doubt that you have got through more money during the past year than the most self-indulgent person I know.'

I looked at Prue as I spoke, but I cannot say that she looked as penitent as I had thought she might. 'I did hope,' I continued, assuming a tone I imagined would touch her to the quick, 'I did hope, my dear, when I went away that you really meant to be more sensible. O, why on earth were you ever christened Prudence? I question whether there is a single penny in the stocking, except the crooked sixpence you put in before I left.'

'That, at any rate, is not there,' said Prudence, her dark eyes dancing with fun. 'I gave it to Johnnie White, whose father beats him so, to buy a new jug in place of one he had just broken in fetching beer for daddy's dinner.'

'And I daresay you gave the stocking too, to some old man with rheumatics! I declare I will go and see!' I started up as I spoke, and ran up-stairs, while Prudence followed, still laughing madly, like the dear little aggravator that she was, and stood in the doorway.

The stocking was there, sure enough, hanging on the same old nail, in the same old spot; but I started back when I saw it, and stood still in utter astonishment. Something in the toe weighed it down far deeper than that old stocking had ever been weighed down in my recollection.

Suddenly a solution occurred to me: 'Stones!' I cried indignantly. 'Ah, Miss Prudence, I am up to your tricks!'

'Stones, indeed!' echoed my cousin, who still stood in the doorway, surveying the scene. 'Take it down, and see.'

I obeyed, and shook the stocking over the snowy counterpane. As I live, out rolled twenty sovereigns!

'Sold for once!' cried Prue as she walked down-stairs, and resumed her needlework.

She tantalised me for some time for my impertinence, but I coaxed her at last into telling me all about her riches. What she told me I will relate, in my own fashion, in the next chapter.

CHAPTER II.

CROSS CRIBBLE.

IN a tumbledown house, situated in a lane leading out of the main street of Handley, there had lived, as long as most of the inhabitants could recollect, a very eccentric old man, named Cribble. That he was rich all agreed; but the reputation of his riches rested only upon hearsay, for except a few bare facts, little was known concerning him, and nothing at all concerning his antecedents. Never had any one crossed his threshold; never had he crossed any one else's, except for his sorry purchases of food and firing at the village shops. As to clothes, during the whole time he had lived at Handley he had never been known to purchase a single garment. Report said he was wearing out the wardrobe of his younger days, which report was certainly fully justified by his appearance. He may, however, have made additions to it of which the Handley gossips knew nothing, during his periodical visits to London, where they said he went to receive his dividends.

Of course, like all such characters, Mr. Cribble had the reputation of being a woman-hater as well as a miser. As to children, so terribly did he scowl and snap, if brought by any chance into contact with them, that he was universally known to the infantine world under the sobriquet of 'Cross Cribble.' The children who had originally bestowed it on him had long since grown to manhood and womanhood; but as the scowl remained, the epithet remained also, and had he lived for centuries, 'Cross Cribble' would to a certainty have been handed down from generation to generation.

It was a lovely afternooon in June, when Prudence carried home a wedding-dress she had just completed for a farmer's daughter in the neighbourhood. Welcome as was the finery itself to the happy girl to whom it symbolised so much, the little dressmaker was almost equally welcomed, and after it had been tried on, and admired by the family, and everybody else within hail of the house, Prudence received her modest guerdon, and with it an invitation to stay tea. Of course she accepted it as heartily as it was given, and she spent an afternoon as happy as kindliness and hospitality, including a grand syllabub in her honour, could make it.

People keep early hours in the country, and

the sun was still shining brightly when she started on her two-mile walk home. But, alas for human pleasure! so quickly that one could hardly have believed so rapid a transition possible, the sky grew overcast, and just as she reached the middle of a meadow, about half a mile from her home, large drops began to patter around her. A ruinous cowshed stood at the further end of the field, and Prudence hastened her steps towards it; for the lightning that began to play around her warned her that she must no longer pursue a path that would lead her in a few paces near a wood of tall trees.

She had only just gained the doorway when a downpour commenced, so heavy that Prudence heartily congratulated herself on her good fortune. Her congratulations were, however, quickly cut short, as Prue perceived a figure crossing the meadow, evidently bent on gaining this same place of shelter, and her heart sank within her when she recognised the bowed head and shambling gait of Cross Cribble. At one time he seemed to swerve from the path, and Prudence drew her breath, thinking perhaps he had not discovered the shed. But it was only for a moment; the next her heart keenly reproached her for her want of charity towards an inoffensive if disagreeable old man; and though she actually trembled at accosting a being who had been the very bugbear of her childhood, she walked as boldly as she could to the door, and made a sign to attract his attention.

So heavy was the rain that, in spite of his age and infirmities, Cribble quickened his pace to a run, until at last he fairly bounded in beside her. He took no notice of her; but began to dry his threadbare clothes with an old tattered blue handkerchief. Her very timidity made her address him.

'It is very wet,' she remarked.

'Humph! I never knew it anything else in a shower. Did you?' he asked, turning on her suddenly.

The angry sarcastic look which accompanied the words so startled our poor little woman that, had the rain been anything short of what it now was, she would probably have run away then and there. As that was not to be thought of, she only gave him a propitiatory smile, and crept as far as she could into the only dry corner the place presented.

Mr. Cribble meantime mounted a large stone which lay under a patch of the roof, a little less pervious to the rain than the rest, steadying himself in his elevation by holding on to a brick in the wall. As he stood looking out through a large opening upon the storm, Prue grew gradually so far reassured that she even began to study his countenance. It was not so very terrible, after all; indeed, had it not been for certain deep lines with which care and calculation had furrowed his cheeks and puckered his forehead, and for a still worse air of low cunning that lurked in his eyes, Christopher Cribble might have been quite a good-looking old man. But as the furrows and the sinister look were there, and as grime and slovenliness were there also, Cross Cribble's *tout ensemble*, to say the least, was not very attractive.

A vivid flash of lightning, followed by a loud clap of thunder, aroused Prudence from her scrutiny, and her whole mind was forthwith absorbed in trying to solve the very puzzling problem—how she was to get home. More and more vivid grew the lightning, louder and louder the thunder, while the rain was now one blinding sheet of water. Never had Prudence witnessed such a storm, and, as she stood and gazed at it with feelings of mingled awe and admiration, she even forgot the presence of the old man, which just before had caused her so much perturbation. She was recalled to it by the sound of his harsh voice addressing her :

' Aren't you frightened ?'

Prue started, and turned to the corner where old Christopher had taken up his position.

' Aren't you frightened ?' he asked again.

' No,' said Prue ; ' I never feel frightened in any danger that comes straight from the hand of God. But, dear me, Mr. Cribble, how wet you are getting ! See, the water is beginning to drip just over where you are standing ; do change places with me, please !'

Old Cribble stared, but said nothing; perhaps he was asking himself whether his favourite theory, that kindness, like everything else, must be bought, could possibly be a falsity after all.

'I am young and strong,' continued Prue, 'and a few drops of rain will do me no harm.'

As she spoke she walked to his side, and, taking him by the arm, helped him gently down from his elevation, and into the place she had hitherto occupied.

Old Cribble made no resistance, but from his new position only stared at her more fixedly than ever. But there was nothing rude or offensive in his gaze. On the contrary, it seemed to Prudence, who caught his eye once or twice, as though half the ugly expression had faded from his face.

'And so you're not frightened ?' he said again at length. 'That's queer; I thought women were frightened at everything. Most of 'em are at me, I know ; and yet I'm sure I never say anything to them. You're a plucky one, you are!' and as he spoke he looked at her with so kindly an expression on his face, that the village children would hardly have recognised Cross Cribble.

Whatever reply Prudence might have made

to this apostrophe was cut short by a flash and simultaneous clap of thunder, which, pealing round them like heavy artillery, shook their place of shelter so violently that pieces of mortar fell from the roof and walls. Prudence uttered an involuntary exclamation, but, after making the sign of the Cross, resumed her quiet attitude.

'What's that?' demanded the old man sharply.

'What's what?' asked Prudence, much startled, and looking round for a rat, snake, or some other dreadfulness.

'Why, what you did just now?'

'What I did? O, I remember; I made the sign of the Cross—this;' and she repeated the sacred symbol.

A strange look passed over Christopher Cribble's face.

'It is many a long day since I did that— yes, many a long day,' he repeated.

'Do you mean that you used to make the sign of the Cross once, yourself?' she asked, bending her large dark eyes upon him.

'Yes, I did, and mother made it too. I have been thinking of her every time you looked at the sky.'

There was a long pause, only broken by a remark from Cribble that the storm was about to abate. It proved to be true: the rain grew less violent, the lightning less vivid, while the thunder subdued to a distant muttering. The stillness was at length broken by Prudence. 'I never knew before that you were a Catholic, Mr. Cribble.'

The lines grew deep as ever, the ugly expression returned in full force.

'Who ever wanted you to know anything about me? I can be what I like, I suppose, eh?'

'Of course,' said Prudence meekly. 'I did not mean—that is to say, I only meant to say, that we Catholics all know each other so well in such a little place as this, and I had never seen you at church; that's all. I beg your pardon, I forgot that perhaps you might go to the Catholic church at W—— or somewhere else, there are so many about here.'

'No, I don't; so you'd better not be perhapsing about me any longer. I don't go anywhere, and don't believe in anything. There, that's my religion, but it's no business of yours.'

'I know; but it was you who first mentioned it by telling me about your mother, if you remember,' said Miss Prue, in a voice the lamb at the stream might have used to the wolf.

'So I did,' said the miser; 'you're right;' and he continued to mutter to himself, while Prudence became so lost in the thought that the wretched old man before her should ever have been a Catholic, that a flash of lightning came unheeded and she made no sign of the Cross.

'Why don't you do it again?' he asked; 'I like to see it. I'm sorry I spoke so rough just now, but I forgot. You see, I'm not used to talk to women, and I don't know how to do it. But do it again, miss, will you? it reminds me of *her*, and I like to see it.'

Reverently enough she complied with his request; then turned on him a smile of such sweet pardon that Christopher Cribble must have been less than man to have spoken roughly to her again.

They had once more relapsed into silence, when suddenly a sound, as of some one crying bitterly outside, broke upon Prue's ear. She walked hastily to the doorway, and looked around, but nothing was to be seen. Thinking it must have been her fancy, Prudence was about to turn away, when the sound broke out afresh, and she soon discovered that it came from a neighbouring hedge. The trusty umbrella that always accompanied her walks was soon up, and Prudence stole on tiptoe over the long wet grass towards the spot whence the sound proceeded.

'Who is there? What is the matter?' she demanded, when arrived within a short distance of the spot.

The answer was the sudden uprisal from a ditch of a shock-head of hair; the next was the somewhat awful apparition of a face beneath it, streaked with blood and tears wherever it was not grimed with dirt. A little body in a very ragged jacket followed next, and disclosed to full view a boy about eleven years of age, who limped towards her.

'Why, Tommy Callaghan, surely that is never you! Why, child, you must be soaked through and through! And dear, dear me, how your poor little leg is bleeding! Here, lean on my arm, and come into this shed, and tell me all about it.'

Of course the sobs redoubled at her words of kindness, and increased almost to a shriek as she lifted the leg of his trousers and disclosed a wound, just below the knee, bleeding copiously.

'Why, Tommy, my man, how did you do it?'

'I was running to get out of the rain, and tumbled on a stone. O dear, O dear! I believe I'll die! I'm sure I'll die of it!'

'Nothing of the sort, Tommy; be still, and see how well I'll make it in two minutes.'

Soothing as was her tone, it had not half as much effect in quieting him as the sudden discovery that Cross Cribble was standing close to his elbow; indeed, a look from that gentleman nipped in the bud one of Tommy's most vociferous complaints.

Prudence commenced her operations by trying to tear her handkerchief in two; alas, fingers and teeth were of no avail! the fabric resisted their utmost efforts.

'Here, take this,' said Cribble, drawing an enormous clasp-knife from his pocket, probably the first act of gratuitous kindness he had performed for at least half a century.

Tommy winced; such an implement in the hand of Cross Cribble, whom he had so often 'cheeked' before running away, was unpleasantly suggestive.

To Tommy's relief, it was soon safe again in the miser's pocket. Then the handkerchief was torn in two; and Prudence, after well washing the wound with one half in a clean little reservoir formed by the rain, bound the leg up tightly with the other. This accomplished, she proceeded to wash Tommy's face, a work of charity that was by no means one of supererogation.

'That's not your boy, is it?' asked Cribble.

'No,' said Prudence, smiling, as she surveyed Tommy's *personnel*, and thought how different her boy should be if she had one. 'No; he belongs to widow Callaghan. You know her, I daresay; she lives in one of Jackson's cottages.'

'I know her!' he exclaimed testily. 'What do you suppose, young woman, I know about her or any other Callaghan? What did that handkerchief cost you?' he asked abruptly.

'I'm sure I don't know!' replied Prudence, opening her eyes.

'That's singular; you bought it, I suppose?'

'I daresay I did, unless it was one of mother's.'

'What do you suppose it cost?'

'Sixpence, perhaps,' said Prue, smiling at his pertinacity.

'And how old are you?'

'Five-and-twenty.'

'Then, young woman, when you get back home, you just do a sum, and you'll see that, by the time you're as old as I am—that's to say, seventy—that sixpence, invested at five per cent compound interest, would have mounted up to some shillings. Now, haven't you been a fool to waste the value of it on a young viper, who'll be breaking your windows, or robbing your apples, the first chance he gets?'

Here Tommy's indignation overruled even his fears of Cross Cribble, and he interposed,

'I'm sure I won't, so there!' The rest was lost in a smothered growl.

'Yes, you will, you little varmint; or somebody like you will, if you don't! People used to tell me when I was young that God never made anything that wasn't of use. Now, I've never yet found out the use of fleas, or fools, or boys. What did God make you for, eh?' he exclaimed, suddenly turning on the boy.

'To know Him, and love Him, and serve Him in this world, and to be happy with Him for ever in the next,' said Tommy.

Whether the answer came in natural sequence to the question, or whether it was prompted by Tommy's Irish wit, Prudence could not say. She only knew that as Tommy turned his face upon his questioner—one of the sweetest boy-faces in the world when clean—and repeated the solemn words, a spasm passed over Cross Cribble's face. It was succeeded by a strange far-away look, and that by two heavy tears. He turned away to hide them.

'Who learned you that, boy?' he asked.

'Father O'Connor,' said Tommy.

'Father Peter learned it to me; but he must have been dead and gone many a long day. Look here, boy. If I gave you a penny, you'd spend it, I suppose?'

'I would,' said Tommy.

'What in?'

Tommy hesitated, such a galaxy of choices hovered before his eyes.

'I know!' he exclaimed at length, with a sigh of relief. 'I'd go shares with Bill Duff, and buy bulls-eyes!'

'A waste of money, generosity, sugar, and everything else!' cried Cribble. 'The bulls-eyes would be forgotten as soon as they were eaten, and Duff would tell lies about you if he's little, or thrash you if he's big, the first chance he got.'

'No, he wouldn't!' cried Tommy; 'and I

don't care if he does! He's my pal, and I'd go shares with him!'

'Fools! fools! fools!' cried Cribble, 'fools one and all!'

He walked to the door as he uttered the words, and looked out. The thunderstorm had altogether ceased, and the rain had subsided into a soft summer shower.

'It's over at last,' he remarked. 'Now, young woman, don't forget to work that sum. Good-day to you.'

'Stop, Mr. Cribble,' said Prudence; 'you had better take my umbrella. You have coughed more than once since you have been here, and people at your age ought not to run risks.'

'And how about your finery?' he asked.

'O, I've nothing on to spoil,' cried Prudence heartily; 'besides, I shall turn my skirt over my head, and get home as dry as a bone. The rain is nothing now.'

'And suppose you meet your young man, how will you like that, eh?' he asked, with a grim smile.

'I haven't one to meet; and he wouldn't know me if I had,' said Prue, 'so it wouldn't matter.'

'And suppose I do take it, young woman, how do you know you'll ever see it back again?'

'You have only to leave it for me with the butcher, and I've faith enough in human nature to know you'll do that. Now, please, take it, Mr. Cribble. I shall consider it as a real kindness, if you will.'

Cribble looked the little pleading face through and through with his piercing eyes.

'Well, I'll take it to please you, and leave it for you at the butcher's. Now, young woman, tell me your name.'

'Prudence Miller.'

'Is that all? Nothing else?'

'Yes; Prudence Mary Miller.'

A nod of the head was the old man's sole reply. He put up the umbrella, turned on his heel, and walked away without any other parting salutation. Prudence looked after him for a minute or two, and then busied herself with turning up her dress for her walk.

'He's a rum cove!' said the boy. 'I knew very well he would never find it in his heart to give me that penny.'

'Yes, he will,' said a voice at the door.

They started. Cross Cribble had returned as suddenly as he had gone.

'Here's the penny, boy; but first say over again what you said just now.'

Tommy repeated the first answer of the Catechism.

'Happy for ever!' muttered the old man, 'happy for ever! And yet they say there's no money there!'

'I tell you what, master,' said Tommy; 'I'll poke my Catechism under your door, and then you can read it all through for yourself if you like.'

'No money there—no money; and yet they say happy for ever!' was the only reply, as Christopher Cribble again turned away, and this time really took his departure.

Prudence and Tommy both watched him out of sight.

'That was a bright idea of yours about the Catechism, Tommy,' said Prudence. 'If you will come round home with me, I will give you a new one, and you shall put it under his door this very night.'

To the indescribable astonishment of Mr. John Moggs, Cross Cribble, the next morning, placed the umbrella in his charge. As time went on he occasionally encountered both Prudence and Tommy in his walks; but he never seemed to recognise either, though the latter, on the strength of the penny, looked his civilest, and tried hard to attract his attention. Summer, autumn, and winter passed away, and Prudence at last gave up all hope of improving the acquaintance so strangely commenced, and which she had at first imagined might have enabled her to minister in some way to the poor lonely old man's necessities, both corporal and spiritual.

But just when the snow and ice had disappeared, and the spring flowers were beginning to peep, a strange whisper ran through the village, at least through the Catholic portion of it, that Cross Cribble had been seen at church. The excitement grew stronger when another whisper came that he had been seen coming out of the confessional. But it reached its acme on Easter Sunday morning, when, in the sight of the whole congregation, a shrinking form with head bowed low was seen creeping up to the Communion-rails, and told the faithful that Christopher Cribble was a Catholic, a wandering sheep safe home again at last in the bosom of the fold.

Whether Prudence's prayers or Tommy's Catechism had anything to do with the happy event nobody ever knew; and as the congregation in general knew nothing about either, they could not well speculate on the subject. For Prudence never talked of other people's affairs, and although Tommy's nature was by no means reticent, he had his own reasons for keeping silent. For chancing to tell his mother about the Catechism directly he had accomplished the feat of pushing it under the door, that prudent matron had advised him to say nothing about it, as otherwise Cross Cribble might some day break his head for meddling; and Tommy Callaghan, for once at least, followed his mother's advice and kept his own counsel.

Not even the forty days of Easter joy did

Christopher Cribble complete on earth. Within three weeks of his Communion he began to break up, and before Ascension-day arrived the old miser had passed away. After his funeral, which was attended by the whole of the Catholic population of Handley, a crowd of relations, young and old, rich and poor, all more or less distantly related, came forward to put in their respective claims for the whole or a portion of his wealth. Great was the disappointment of each and all when they learned that, with the exception of two small legacies, the whole had been left to a Catholic orphanage in the vicinity. Of the two legacies, the one was a sum sufficient to apprentice Thomas Callaghan to any trade he might choose; the other was a sum of 'twenty pounds, free of legacy duty, to Prudence Mary Miller, spinster, for lending an old man her umbrella, and walking home in the rain herself.'

CHAPTER III.

IN SPITE OF MYSELF.

'WELL, my dear Prue,' said I, when my cousin had concluded her story, which I need not say was not related precisely as I have given it, 'well, my dear, and so I may congratulate you at last upon being rich. What a lucky girl you are! How I wish I could meet some such old crosspatch in my rambles! He should be kindly welcome to my very best umbrella, I can tell you, if he would pay me as handsomely for the loan of it. Twenty pounds comes in conveniently, one may say.'

'I do so wish you would take it, dear; you want it so much more than I do, with that terrible loss you have had through that bad, bad French teacher.'

I folded her in my arms and kissed her, as I always did when she was silly. She knew as well as if I had spoken that that hug and kiss meant no, and so tried a compromise.

'Well, take half. Do let us share it, Esther; it will make me so happy. Let us each put 10*l.* in our old stockings, and see who will add most to it.'

'No, no, no! Now listen, my most cousinly cousin,' said I, assuming the air of superiority to which my five years' seniority entitled me: 'I thank you and love you all the same, but I am not going to touch your money. I have the hands and the health to labour for myself; and when these begin to fail I shall fall back upon my great expectations, which, perhaps, by that time, in all human probability, will be realised, seeing that I am still young, and my poor aunt nearly eighty. No, Prue, my dear, I want to see you laying by for a rainy day. Go on filling your stocking; it will not be difficult with such a substantial nest-egg. That will really give me greater pleasure than anything else I know.'

Prue looked disappointed, but said no more; and, after hanging up the stocking on its usual nail, we went down-stairs to get dinner, and were soon both busily engaged in the concoction of a gooseberry pudding.

The next morning two letters came addressed to Miss Prudence Miller, the one by post, the other by the grubby but trusty hand of Master Tommy Callaghan. The first, which was from our uncle Gregory, a personage much feared and respected by us both, as the grandee of the family, Prue read, and handed to me. It ran as follows:

'My dear Prudence,—A customer of mine, who was present at the reading of the late Mr. Christopher Cribble's will, tells me he has left you 20*l*. I congratulate you, my dear niece; for to any one in your humble position this money, properly invested, will be quite a little fortune. I only know, thanks to my parents' partiality for my sisters, I had to commence life on very little more, though that's neither here nor there. I expect to be at Handley some time during the summer or autumn; and you had better do nothing with your money till you see me, as I know of an investment that will just suit you.

It is very money-making and perfectly safe, or I wouldn't, you may be sure, advise you to it. Accept my love.—Your affectionate uncle,
　　　　　　　　　'GREGORY FARLEY.'

'Well now, Prue,' said I, 'that is just the very thing. I was so wishing uncle Gregory would advise you about this money, but I was afraid the sum was too small to trouble him with; and now, you see, he himself offers to help you. Isn't it grand?'

'Yes,' said Prue, but very absently, as she laid the other letter in her lap.

'Because, you see, although they say he is a little sharp in his bargains with strangers, I am sure he would act conscientiously with his own niece.'

'Yes,' said Prue again.

'I wish you would promise me not to do anything with your money till you see him. Will you?'

Prue started, and ceased to contemplate the white rose-bush at the further end of the back garden.

'Will I do what?'

'Only promise me not to do anything with your money till uncle Gregory comes—that is to say, unless something quite unforeseen occurs.'

Prue smiled.

'And in that case?'

'Why, of course, you must act according to the necessity of the moment. For instance, if you were to break your leg, or catch scarlet fever, or get burned out of house and home, these would, of course, be the very consequences for which money ought to be saved up.'

'I am afraid, though, in the latter case the money might get burned too,' said Prue, laughing. 'Well, something unforeseen has occurred. Read that;' and she pushed the second letter, which had been lying open in her lap ever since she had finished reading it, towards me.

'Whom is it from?' I asked, half angry, yet at the same time half frightened.

'Do you remember Mrs. Forsyth, who used to keep the little wool-shop?'

'Of course I do. Has she left it?'

'Yes, some months since. I don't know whether you ever heard her history. She is almost a lady by birth and education, and her husband was captain of a large merchant-vessel. After his death she became a Catholic, and the executors, who were bigoted Dissenters, at once made a new arrangement about her property, so that her yearly income was reduced to much less than half. With Father O'Connor's help she opened the wool-shop here, but latterly it was too much for her to manage. She gave it up just about the time mother died, and went to live in apartments. Almost directly after that, another alteration was made about the property. The last remaining executor, who had always manifested especial ill-will towards her from the moment of her conversion, on some excuse or another, threw the property into Chancery, and thus deprived her straight away of even the little income she possessed. I have heard that he imagined it would drive her back again, but he was mistaken. She was left quite suddenly with no provision but half-a-crown a week from a different source, which, until this time, she had always devoted to charity. At first she thought, and we all thought, that she would only be subjected to a temporary inconvenience; but we all know what "getting into Chancery" means, though I believe the law has been altered of late, and perhaps she may even yet live to get back her money; but at present she is in a pitiful state. I had no idea of it, poor dear old soul; just read what she says, Esther.'

I read aloud:

'Dear Prudence,—I hardly know why I tell you my troubles, since I know well, poor child, how impossible it is for you to help me, except by your prayers and sympathy, and perhaps your good advice. Dear Prudence, I have been trying to live on the half-a-crown a week, all that is left of my income, but I can do so no longer. My room costs me a shilling a week out of it, and the rest goes a very little way in providing all the other necessaries of life, to say nothing of those of old age, and I am nearly starving. They tell me now my law business may take a year to settle, and so the workhouse alone lies before me. Even there I cannot go in peace, for I owe that poor dear little Mrs. Thompson five pounds, which I cannot, cannot pay. Both she and I felt so certain I should be getting my money long before the year was out, that when she pressed me to continue to get my things of her I yielded to the temptation, though directly I knew what I know now I refused to have anything else. Now, don't be coming to offer me your hardly-earned gains, but come and talk over my troubles with me, like the dear little consoler that you are. They are great indeed, but they have been already carried for me along the Way of the Cross, and I cannot murmur.—Your loving friend,   MARGARET FORSYTH.'

'What do you think of that, Esther?' asked Prue, as, without a word, I laid the second letter on the top of the first. 'Am I to promise now not to touch the twenty pounds?'

'Yes, indeed you are; for if you once touch that you will never begin to save. I have brought more money than I want, and I can very well spare you ten shillings for Mrs. Forsyth;' and I began to fumble for my purse.

'I thank you and love you all the same; but I am not going to touch your money,' said Prue, exactly mimicking my words and manner of the day before. 'Besides, my dear, ten shillings would be comparatively useless in such a case as this.'

It was impossible to deny that, so I only asked meekly what Prue proposed doing.

'Paying off the five pounds, and bringing Mrs. Forsyth home here to live with me. I want a mother and she wants a home, so nothing could be better. Two are kept almost as cheaply as one, and her half-a-crown a week will make her feel quite independent in other things. If ever her money comes back to her we may make a different arrangement, but till then it must be as I propose.'

'Will she not be a tie to you?' I asked.

'Yes,' said Prudence, with her eyes full of tears, 'I shall feel tied once again to something motherly, sweet, and pious. Now, Esther, I know very well you are the last on earth to discourage this investment of the money our Lord Himself has sent me to invest.'

Thank God, she spoke the truth. I dared not, at that moment, have uttered another word of worldly prudence to my unworldly Prue, to save my life.

'It will be the more delightful to pay Mrs. Thompson the five pounds, because I know she wants it,' continued Prue, 'for her rent. She told me last night she was terribly in want of poor Mrs. Forsyth's money, but that she could not find it in her heart to mention it to her. So now, you see, this expenditure of five pounds will make three people happy. Is not that better than letting it lie a lump, that rust and moth might corrupt, and thieves break through and steal?'

'I have no more to say,' said I. 'Prudence, I don't believe that, ever before, a woman—'

'Had a head on her shoulders, I suppose,' said Prue; 'because I am sure that is the only thing that can be said of me; and as I never heard of one born without, that is not much of a distinction, after all. But now, Esther, you will have to take my part against uncle Gregory. He will storm finely, I expect, when he finds only fifteen pounds left.'

'Trust me,' I replied; 'I never allow anybody to scold you but myself! When are you going to see Mrs. Forsyth?'

'I meant to have gone this afternoon, but I think we had better go at once; for I don't think either you or I could enjoy our dinner, Esther, while she is sitting in that wretched room without one. I say we, for I think you would like to go too, dear.'

'I should indeed, very much. Shall we start now?'

'Wait a moment. Listen, Esther. Would you very much mind giving up your room, and coming to sleep with me? and then Mrs. Forsyth could come to us at once. You would like that, wouldn't you, dear?'

Somehow my eyes must have given consent, for I was too much pleased to say a word, and so was Prudence; so, by way of showing our pleasure, we both burst into tears and had a good cry.

That was a visit! I shall never forget the poor bare sunless little room, nor the emaciated face that was looking listlessly, when we entered, into a wretched back yard, filled with all kinds of house lumber, and any number of dirty, rude, noisy children. Even now I can see Prue kneeling at the old lady's feet, whispering all she wished her to understand in the softest accents, for fear the joy should be too much for her, while I sat on the bed, the only other seat in the room, too happy even to think. It was long before the old lady could be brought to accept Prudence's offer. She had heard nothing of the legacy, and the account of it seemed so incredible that she thought we must be making the story up to induce her to accept the gift. Her persuasion that money must be coming to her soon, and therefore that she might conscientiously regard the whole as a loan, at length induced her to consent. I may, however, add parenthetically that, though many a long day has passed since Mrs. Forsyth took her departure for a better world, that business is still in Chancery, still unsettled.

But Chancery had nothing to do with our affairs, at any rate; and nobody else seemed inclined to put difficulties in our way. A small arrear of rent rather bothered us all three at first; but when we called in the landlady, she agreed at once to take the few articles of furniture left in the room in lieu of it. So, leaving the old lady's single trunk to be brought by Tommy, we started for Prue's cottage, and, though we had had so much to talk over and arrange, it was still quite early in the afternoon when we reached it. I say we; for, though I stopped on the way to pay Mrs. Thompson's bill, I caught them up at the garden-gate, and had the joy of helping to welcome dear old Margaret Forsyth to her new home.

Under our united care she soon grew quite well again, and, with returning health, recovered that flow of spirits that had once made her little shop the sunniest spot in the village. When, at the end of my bright happy holiday, I returned once more to my pupils and pianos, my anxiety about Prudence was very much lightened now that she had Mrs. Forsyth to bear her company. I loved to picture her with that cheery old face *vis-à-vis* to hers, and that kindly grateful old heart ready to sympathise with her in all the little daily worries and troubles that I knew must come to Prudence Miller, as they come to each and all of us.

But I am anticipating. Only one week of my holiday had gone as yet; I had still three more to spend with my darling.

CHAPTER IV.

ANOTHER INVESTMENT.

'ESTHER, my dear, will you do the marketings for me?' asked Prue one morning, about a week after Mrs. Forsyth's arrival. Now, if there was anything I loved it was a morning ramble, in and out and round about those quaint little shops, and a free and easy gossip with the still quainter country people behind the various counters, and I consented with alacrity. I was the more satisfied that it was not often Prue thus commissioned me. I somehow fancy that my operations in the bargaining line were not quite as satisfactory to her as they appeared to me.

I returned home with a basketful of good

things, and was looking for Prudence, when I heard the sound of voices in the parlour, the door of which was shut. Making sure that Prue was trying on a dress, as she often did in that room, I put my purchases on the kitchen table, and ran up-stairs to the bedroom I now shared with her, to take off my things. To my surprise, Miss Prue was there *in propriâ personâ*, arranging, or rather rearranging, the curtains of the bed (for I myself had made it, and dusted the room, before going out). It was strange that Prue should be thus occupied, with customers or visitors waiting down-stairs, thought I; but the look on Prue's face—nervous, mischievous, and comical all in one—was stranger still, and I at once asked her what was the matter.

'Nothing, my dear; how absurd you are! What can be the matter?'

'Prue,' said I, 'you look as guilty as if you had been stealing. O Prue,' I exclaimed, as a sudden suspicion flashed across me, 'I do believe you have been robbing your own stocking! O Prue, how can you?' I exclaimed, quite pathetically.

A merry laugh was the only reply as I took down the article in question, and again emptied it on the bed. Alas, my fears were confirmed! Eight pounds and a wretched little half-sovereign alone remained.

'Six-pound-ten at a swoop!' I cried; and I verily believe tears of vexation stood in my eyes as I spoke.

'Well, I can't stop to tell you now about it, my dear, because Jenny Foster is waiting for me down-stairs.'

'Jenny Foster, indeed!' I exclaimed. 'I suppose you mean Polly?'

'No, I don't, I mean Jenny; though Polly is there too, for the matter of that.'

'Jenny Foster!' I repeated, utterly aghast; for only a day or two before I had stood by the side of her bed, which she now rarely left, except to sit up for a short time in a large armchair in her room.

'I will tell you all about it afterwards,' said Prue; 'I must go now. Come down and see her, will you?'

I followed, still quite bewildered, to the parlour, where, sure enough, I found Jenny Foster, a pretty girl of eighteen, apparently far gone in consumption, seated on the sofa, propped up by pillows. Her mother and sister were with her, and wished me a cordial good-morning; but directly Jenny tried to speak her words died away into an hysteric sob.

'There, there, dear; don't try and talk, but drink some of this nice hot wine-and-water,' said Prudence. 'Be quick, or Father O'Connor will be back with the chair. Jenny and her mother are going to London, Esther. Mr. Blackie has said all along that hers is not real consumption, and he is hopeful that if she can only be put for a time under Dr. ——, who has done such wonders in similar cases, she may come back to us again quite well.'

'Won't the journey be too much for her?' I asked the mother.

'I hope not. We are choosing to-day, because Father O'Connor is going to London for his holiday, and he will take care of us. God bless him! He says he will never leave us till he sees us safe in the convent, where his sister is a nun, and where they have offered to take us free of all expense. He has gone now to borrow old Mrs. Crump's Bath-chair to take Jenny to the station.'

'Isn't he good?' exclaimed Jenny faintly; 'and aren't the nuns good, too? Still, notwithstanding all their kindness, I couldn't have gone, Esther, if it had not been for dear, dear Prudence! Isn't she an angel?' And she seized the hand that had just conveyed a spoonful of wine-and-water to her mouth, and kissed it rapturously, teaspoon and all.

'Silly, silly child!' cried Prudence, disengaging her hand, and shaking her finger at her. 'It is clear enough you have never been saint enough to see an angel, or you would know better what they're like! Never mind, I won't scold you now; but wait till you come back, well and strong, that's all!'

At this moment Father O'Connor entered, and told us that the chair was outside, furnished with shawls, biscuits, brandy, and everything else proper—and improper—to an invalid that kind Mrs. Crump could lay hands on at a moment's notice. After any amount of good wishes and lingering good-byes, the travellers took their leave, and Mrs. Forsyth and I stood watching them at the window. As to Prudence, she had, of course, insisted on going with them to the station to see them off, and bring poor lonely Polly back with her to dinner.

'I wonder how it was that Prudence never told me a word of all this?' I remarked to the old lady.

'She was afraid, my dear, that you would be so grieved and worried at seeing the money go that you would very naturally try and advise her not to help them. And no wonder either, my dear. Six-pound-ten to them and five pounds for me has, indeed, made a hole in the poor child's little fortune.'

'But yours is only a loan, you know,' I said soothingly.

'Yes, only a loan; I shall hope to pay the dear girl back, with interest, in less than a year, for all I am costing her now. But you see, my dear, nothing less than what Prudence has given

the Fosters would have been of any use. The
railway journey will be so expensive, because
they have had to engage two places, and put a
board across, for poor Jenny; and they will have
so many other expenses, with one thing and
another (although Mr. Blackie has written to
Dr. ——, and he thinks he will charge them
comparatively little), that it is pretty sure it will
cost them quite ten pounds. Now, Prue somehow found out, a day or two ago, that, do what
they might, they could only muster three-pound-
ten, so she told Father O'Connor she would
make it up. She wanted him to take it to them
as his own gift; but he said, and very properly
too, that he was not going to have the credit of
other people's good works. Although she did
not know they were leaving so soon, she was all
day yesterday trying to make up some excuse
for going in to see them without you, but could
not manage it. This morning she sent you out
marketing on purpose to get rid of you; and
just as you had gone, Father O'Connor and
Polly brought Jenny in, because she insisted on
thanking Prudence herself. Prue slipped the
money into Father O'Connor's hand when he
came back with the chair, far more pleased to
get rid of it than she was, I'll be bound, when
the news of the legacy came to her. The one
drawback to her happiness has been her regret
at disappointing you; and it is, indeed, a pitiful

thing to think that more than half her legacy has gone in about a fortnight.'

'The darling!' I exclaimed enthusiastically. 'No, not gone, only invested. Do tell her, dear Mrs. Forsyth, that I am every bit as contented and happy about it all as she is. Dear little Prue! I am sure she ought to be canonised!'

'You had better not tell her so, or she will say that you know as little about saints as Jenny does about angels. Besides, we shall have to wait till she is dead, you know; and God forbid that I, at least, may live for that!'

CHAPTER V.

A BRUISED REED.

'PRUDENCE MILLER, I am going to ask you a favour,' said Mrs. Anderson, our next-door neighbour, putting her head over the garden-wall. Prue, who was gathering peas, immediately put the basket into my hand, and hastened forward to hear what it might be.

'My Jim is coming home to-morrow for his week's holiday, as you know,' continued Mrs. Anderson, with a bright happy look. 'Now, isn't it tiresome? I have just got a letter from my brother, asking me if I can put him up with his wife and two children for a couple of nights. They think a run into the country would do

the little ones good. Now, I don't want to be
disobliging; besides, I should dearly like 'em to
see my Jim, for they've never set eyes on him
since he was ten years old; but what can I do?
Where can I put 'em all? says I to Mrs. Stocks;
houses isn't made of indy-rubber, you know.
Well, now, Mrs. Stocks put it into my head to
ask you if so be you could make a bed up for
Jim for a night or two on your sofy?'

'With pleasure, Mrs. Anderson, for the whole
time he is here, if you like. I was so pleased
yesterday when I heard that Jim was coming;
he is such a favourite of mine; he was always
such a straightforward well-mannered boy. He
does you credit, Mrs. Anderson;' and Prudence
gave the proud and happy mother one of those
heart-smiles that I often think went further than
anything else in making her such a universal
favourite. 'How is he getting on in his place?'
she asked.

'O, famously. I've had my troubles, as you
know, better perhaps than most folks; sorrow
upon sorrow, till my heart has almost broke;
but I do think my Jim will be a real comfort to
me, and so does Father O'Connor. He really
ought, when you remember that he is the only
one left to me out of six.'

'And so he will, dear Mrs. Anderson,' said
Prue.

'I am sure I hope so; they say Mr. Green

thinks all the world of him—blessed be God! Well, I must be going, for I've a power of things to do inside. Thank you very much, Prudence, about the bed; I'm so much obliged to you.'

Jim duly made his appearance the next night, and, after sitting a little while with us in the kitchen, retired into the parlour, to take possession of the snug little bed Prue and I had arranged for him. After all I had heard in his favour from Prudence and others, I must say I was disappointed in our visitor. Thin almost to gauntness, and pale almost to sallowness, with a downcast eye, a fitful timid glance, and a nervous twitching of the mouth, it required more imagination than I possessed to realise that James Anderson had ever been good-looking, although his features were certainly well cut and regular, and his figure tall and shapely. Nor were the genial frank manners, of which I had heard so much, anywhere discernible in those of the morose absent-minded youth, who only answered Prue's friendly questions and remarks with monosyllables.

'How ill he looks!' said Prue, as we heard the parlour-door close upon him.

'Yes,' said Mrs. Forsyth, as she lighted her bedroom candle, 'if there were consumption in that family, I should say poor Jimmy was doomed.'

'I never heard of any,' said Prudence. 'Mrs.

Anderson has been unfortunate in her children, but they all either died of fever or of convulsions in teething. Her husband was a strong healthy man when he met with that accident, of which he really died in the end.'

'He was,' said Mrs. Forsyth. 'Poor Jim! Well, I can't say I like the looks of him. Good-night, my dears;' and the old lady retired after a kiss to both of us.

It was still early, and Prue and I remained up working, and chatting quietly of old times.

'Whatever is that?' exclaimed my cousin, suddenly breaking off an anecdote she was telling me.

She might well ask, so strange and wild was the cry that reached our ears. We both started up to listen, and found that it came from the next room. We were soon at the parlour-door, and stood there for some little time; but the voice had ceased, and, except for a deep groan, all was silent. After listening awhile we were about to retire, when Jim recommenced,

'Don't! don't! I tell you I didn't do it! I won't go with you, I tell you! leave me alone! He made me do it! there he is! take him! take him!'

'He is dreaming,' said I.

'Mother, mother, don't look like that! I couldn't help it! indeed, I couldn't!' cried the sleeper, after a pause.

'If he goes on much longer I shall walk in and wake him, that I shall,' said Prue, laying her hand on the door. 'Dear me, what a pity, he has bolted it inside!'

We returned after a while to the kitchen, and soon after went up-stairs to bed. We could still hear Jim's voice at intervals, but it was not near enough to disturb us, and after a few remarks about him and sleep-talkers in general, we both feel asleep.

He was to come in to supper with us the next evening, and Prue had asked one of his old friends to meet him. As we had made up his bed early, we had supper in the kitchen. A bright little fire rendered it the most cosy spot in the house that evening, for the weather was wet and chilly, more like October than July. It all looked so bright, I remember, with the firelight shining on the tins and coppers, and dancing on the plates and glasses that were laid for supper. With the exception of Jim, who was moody as ever, we were a very merry party; for Andrew Phillips was in his best possible spirits, and he and Mrs. Forsyth kept up such a running fire of fun, that Prudence and I laughed till the tears came. Jim took no part in the merriment, but sat looking from one to the other of the speakers with the sickliest of sickly smiles upon his lips; just such a smile as that Spartan boy must have worn who watched the national games with the stolen fox beneath his garment, secretly gnawing him to death.

Andrew went soon after supper, and we all prepared to retire for the night.

'You had bad dreams last night, I am afraid, Jim,' said Prue, as she handed him a candle.

'How do you know?' he asked almost sharply.

'Because you gave us the benefit of them,' said my cousin, laughing; 'you called out so loudly that Esther and I were quite frightened. I am afraid you must have had too good a supper last night, Jim.'

'You must take care, or we shall learn all your secrets,' added I.

Never shall I forget the effect of that speech, which I intended should be jocose. His hair seemed almost to rise from his head, and his face to break out into a cold perspiration.

'My secrets? my secrets? Who told you I had any, I should like to know?' he demanded quite fiercely.

I started back, terrified at his vehemence, but Prue came to the rescue.

'Nonsense, Jim! Can't you see that Esther is in fun? Why, old man, whatever is coming over you?'

'Nothing,' replied the boy, 'nothing. I haven't been well lately, that is all. I didn't mean to speak so sharp;' and he looked at me so sweetly and sorrowfully that I began to understand Prue's partiality for him.

'Well, go to bed now, Jim,' said my cousin. 'You look as if you want rest. What a large bundle!' she added. 'Why, Jim, you want more for a night than I should for a week.'

Again a terrible look shot across his face; but muttering something about liking to change his clothes, he disappeared for the night, locking the parlour-door with a click that seemed to say what an intense relief it was to him to put a barrier between himself and the outer world.

'Esther,' said Prue, when we reached our room, 'it is only ten, and I am not at all sleepy. I think I will sit up a little time, and work at this frock. They want it as soon as I can get it done. Now, don't you mind me, but go to bed and go to sleep. I shall not be long after you.'

'I would rather help you,' said I, as I tried to suppress a yawn that would come. 'I am quite wide awake.'

'You look so,' said Prue. 'No, my dear, go to bed, like a good child. Awake, indeed! you can hardly keep your eyes open.'

'Well, anyway, I won't go to bed till you do, but I will just lie down a little on the outside of the quilt. I sha'n't go to sleep.'

But the figure of my cousin stitching away for her life, by her shaded lamp, soon grew hazy, and I did go to sleep—for how long, I know not, nor do I know what woke me; but I did wake up after a time, to see Prue, with a startled look on her face, listening attentively. I was about to speak, but a finger on her lip enjoined silence.

'What is it?' asked my eyes.

Prue crossed the room on tiptoe.

'Somebody trying the front-door, I think. Don't be frightened; you know we have Jimmy in the house. Stay quiet; I am going to creep down-stairs to listen.'

'Take the light,' I whispered.

'Goose! It would scare them away; and I want to know if there is really any one there.' And she glided from the room, partly closing the door behind her.

I sat up on the bed and listened, too sick, between my fears and sudden awakening, to do anything else. For, reader dear, I am a terrible coward—quite a different sort of person from my brave little Prue.

But I did not sit there long. First, I distinctly heard a door open down-stairs, then an exclamation, then a fall, and then a sudden cry from Prue, begging me to come. I may say for myself that my cowardice vanished at once as I pictured my darling half-murdered by robbers; and seizing the lamp, and tearing off its shade, I rushed down-stairs. The lamp revealed the very reverse of the scene I had pictured; for there stood Prue, white indeed, but still her own calm self, supporting, or rather trying to support, the body of a man who was fast slipping from her grasp.

'Here, Esther, here! help me to hold him. Don't let him fall, and don't wake Mrs. Forsyth —it's only Jimmy!'

It was indeed Jimmy, but in such a deadly swoon that, when I first looked at him, I thought he must be dead. With considerable difficulty we dragged him into the kitchen, and propped him up with his own bundle, that I found on the floor in the passage. Then we untied his necktie, for he was fully dressed, and tried, with every restorative we could lay hands on, to revive him.

'How did it happen? where did you find him?' I asked, as I chafed his blue cold hands.

'As I stood in the passage,' said Prudence, 'that was just very faintly lighted from our room, I heard him moving about, and listened. Presently I saw his door open, and he came out, fully dressed, with his hat on, and his bundle under his arm. He stood still for a moment, as soon as he saw the light in our room; but it looked so like the flicker of a night-light, and the house was so still, that he seemed satisfied. He went to the street-door, and had just undone the top bolt, when I laid my hand on his arm. He only gave one low cry, and then fainted dead away, as you see him.'

'He must have meant to run away, and that was why he brought his bundle,' said I. 'How dreadful! Hadn't I better run for his mother?'

'No, wait a bit; it will give her such a fright,' said Prudence. 'Besides, I think he is beginning to revive.'

Sure enough, almost as she spoke, Jimmy heaved a sigh; and the moment after, tossing up his arms, began to rave wildly.

'Yes, yes! take me! I am ready! I took the money! take me, take me! I am ready! Anything better than this dog's life!'

'Hush, Jim, hush!' said Prue gently, but turning deadly pale. 'Hush! there is nobody here but Esther and me. Don't talk like that!'

He opened his eyes and looked at her, and gradually seemed to take in the situation. He raised himself to a sitting position, and looked around.

'I have told you my secrets now,' he said, with a bitter smile; 'and you can do what you like with them.'

'I shall first do what I like with you,' said Prudence; 'and, after that, if you like to confide your troubles to Esther and me—both old, old friends of your mother, Jim—you shall. But don't speak of anything, or even think of anything, till we have brought a little bit of colour back again into that pale face.'

She poked up the embers of the fire as she

spoke, put in a few chips, that were soon blazing brightly, and set on the kettle. Then we wheeled an old settee to the fire, on which we managed to dispose our invalid, whose face already, to my thinking, began to wear a softer expression. At this moment the voice of old Mrs. Forsyth was heard, calling from the stairs to know what was the matter.

'Only that Jim Anderson has been a little poorly, but he is much better now.'

'I thought there was something wrong about him, that I did,' we heard the old lady mutter to herself. 'Shall I dress, and come down?'

'No, dear,' said Prue; 'only let me have a little of that brandy I put in your cupboard, and then go to sleep again. I promise to let you know if he is worse.'

The kettle was soon boiling, and a steaming glass of brandy-and-water quickly brought the life once more into the poor boy's frame. As soon as we saw him better we began to smile, and, strange to say, that was the signal for him to go off into a passionate burst of tears. Prudence soon calmed him with her own quiet tact, and then, side by side, we sat and listened to all he chose to tell us. The morning sun was shining brightly into our bedroom before Prue and I went to bed.

It would weary the reader were I to relate all Jimmy told us. I will only say it was a very sad story indeed—a story of an infatuated affection for a designing youth in every way unworthy of it; of a swerving from honesty, for which a desire to save a friend might be alleged, but never could be accepted, as an excuse. A sad, sad story of a boy foolishly blind to the faults of another, and sinking deeper and deeper every day into dishonesty and fraud for his sake; a story with a bitter, yet salutary, moral in the black ingratitude of him for whom all this had been risked—a practical application of the good old proverb, 'The devil's wheat is all chaff.'

'And do you really mean to say, Jimmy, that you have suffered all this, although you have never appropriated to your own use any of your master's money?'

'I do indeed, Prudence. Every pound I took, every figure I falsified, was to save Reginald from disgrace and ruin. He told me he would pay it all back almost immediately, and I waited for him night after night on the old spot. At last I heard that he had left for Australia, without any word but the message that told me he was gone.'

'And where were you going when I touched you?' asked Prudence.

'Anywhere—to Liverpool, I think, because I could have got a ship from there better than anywhere else; and my only thought has been to get away from the police. And I must go directly!' he cried, suddenly starting up, while his face contracted with the old expression of fear; 'I must go directly, or they will be after me even here; and that would kill my poor dear mother, I know it would. I would never have run the risk of it, but I felt I must see my mother just once more. O Prudence Miller, do be good to her, and make her understand I was not quite a common thief!'

There was a long pause, broken only by his sobs.

'How much money did you take, Jim? You have not told me that,' said Prue at length.

'Ten pounds.'

A simultaneous exclamation from us both made him look up.

'It may not seem so much to you, but it is more than I could make up in a year on my wages; and the books will be overhauled in a week or two, if they haven't done it already,' he added, in a voice of agony.

'Jim,' began my cousin, 'God knows I would not call any sum dishonestly acquired a small one, in the sense of its being a small sin before either God or man. I do, moreover, think that stealing in any shape, or for anybody's sake, is a crime so terrible that every one who commits it ought to be punished. You have certainly incurred the guilt, but you have also endured the punishment; and I think, dear Jimmy, it is over now, for God has put it in my power to give you the ten pounds.'

'You, Prudence!'

'Yes, I; that is to say,' she added, 'all but ten shillings, and that—' She looked at me.

'Is here and waiting,' I answered so promptly, as I pulled out my purse, that Prue declared she was certain that half-sovereign would have burnt a hole if it had remained any longer in my pocket. Pretty cool, I thought, from one who had heard so many homilies from me on the subject of saving.

In another minute a little rouleau of ten pounds was lying on Jim's palm, and I actually joined Prudence in crying for joy, though the old gray stocking lay on the table beside us flat as a pancake.

CHAPTER VI.

UNCLE GREGORY'S VISIT.

A DAY or two after that memorable night my holiday came to an end, and I returned once more to my usual haunts and daily occupation; and a weary occupation it seemed at first, after my *dolce far niente* life among the sweet green fields of Handley, as I trudged from school to school through the noisy streets, in the broiling heat of a London August. Happily for me, it grew less and less weary every day, as I once again grew accustomed to its monotony, and as each hour drew me nearer to a sunny prospect that, amid all my weariness, was ever dancing before my eyes. For Prudence had promised to come and spend a week with me in the beginning of September, and I was contriving to give extra lessons at all the places I attended, that I might have my time free during her stay. Of course, I had to work hard—so hard that more than one of my employers told me I should lose all the benefit I had gained by my holidays; but not one ever abated a jot or tittle of her requirements, for all that.

The extra lessons came to an end at last, and the very next day Prue made her appearance at my lodgings, fresh and bonnie as the bouquet she brought me. Now, I have said so much about my visit to her that the reader's patience would utterly fail were I to begin upon her visit to me. Besides, she came, of course, at a time when London is out of town; and, however enchanting it might seem to Prue, my friends in general were dubbing it 'exceedingly slow.' So I will not drag the reader as I dragged Prue, from the Polytechnic to Madame Tussaud's, from the Agricultural to the Albert Hall, from the Thames Tunnel to the Tower, and from one deserted park to another. One afternoon, however, I must exempt from the rest, and that was the one upon which we were expecting uncle Gregory, who, having failed to pay his projected visit to Handley, had now written to say he would run over and spend an hour with us in Pimlico instead.

It was the first time he had ever honoured my humble home with a visit, although his residence was only an omnibus journey from mine, and of course we both knew that he was coming about the twenty pounds, and of course we were both terribly frightened. If he had left us the time we should have written in desperation, and told him the truth, and so prevented his coming; but the letter only arrived an hour or two before we were to expect him, and so there was nothing for it but to submit to our fate with the best grace we could. One hope alone remained: Father O'Connor had run up to London on business, and had sent us word he would call in on his way back to Victoria. If he should only chance to come in at the same time as uncle Gregory, what a shield and buckler he would be against the assaults of the enemy! Unfortunately, however, we had heard, from our respective mothers, that uncle Gregory was proverbially prompt and punctual; while, alas! we knew from experience that Father O'Connor was almost always late.

'What will you give him for tea, my dear?' I asked Prue. Of course the *him* meant uncle

Gregory, for we had talked of nothing else ever since the ran-tan of the midday post.

'Something that takes a long time to eat, I think,' said I, 'because I don't suppose he will want to begin upon business till after tea, and that will give us more chance of Father O'Connor.'

'Well, what does take a long time to eat?' said Prue reflectively. 'Tough steaks and captain's biscuits are both difficult to manage, but we couldn't well give him either of those!'

'No,' said I, shaking my head, 'neither of them is exactly proper for tea; besides, perhaps he hasn't many teeth at his age. Prue!' added I, glowing with a sudden inspiration, 'what do you think of shrimps?'

'Capital!' cried my cousin, 'just the very thing! Besides, they will look so nice on one side of the table, with a plate of watercresses on the other. Let me run out and get them while you lay the tea-things, for he will be here almost directly.'

The table was just laid, and we ourselves arrayed in best bib and tucker, when the great man arrived. Great, indeed, for my poor little cane chair groaned and creaked under his weight. Indeed, I question, dear reader, whether you or I ever saw a much bigger man than my uncle Gregory; and I may add—as you are never likely to know him, and turn his niece's admission to her disadvantage—a much more disagreeable one. He was civil, but stiff as a poker; wished us good-day, and inquired shortly and snappishly after one or two people at Handley; then sat down, with his hands in his pockets, looking us through and through every time we spoke, and jerking out monosyllables in reply. He was so truly uncomfortable that, although we had planned to delay the making of the tea as long as possible, I put it in the pot at once, and cut short the sitting by taking my place at the table.

To our intense disgust, uncle Gregory refused the shrimps, pronouncing them 'a waste of time, and not worth the trouble of picking!' But he ate muffins and watercresses like an ogre, only pausing in the operation to swallow huge gulps of the tea he had poured into his saucer. He was evidently a man, who looked upon his meals as part of the business of life, and before Prue or I had shelled and despatched a dozen of the tempting little crustacea, he had finished. Having pushed back his cup and saucer, and pulled out and consulted an enormous watch, uncle Gregory proceeded to business.

'And now, Prudence, with regard to this money.'

Of course we relinquished our cups and saucers and unfinished dainties; and pushing back our chairs, and settling our dresses, prepared to listen. I only know if Prue felt as I did, she had never felt so miserable in her life before.

'With regard to this money,' he repeated somewhat severely; for the interruption caused by our movement had not been lost upon him, 'the investment of such a small—'

'Uncle,' said Prue faintly.

'Will you please allow me to finish without interruption what I was going to say? I was about to observe, madam,' he continued, scowling at Prue from under his shaggy eyebrows, 'that the investment of such a small sum of money as twenty pounds is, as a rule—'

'But, uncle, dear uncle—' said poor Prue, terrified at interrupting him, yet still more terrified at the consequences of letting him proceed with his very fruitless harangue.

'If you *can* be quiet for a couple of minutes, Miss Prudence Miller, I really shall be very much obliged. How strange it is that you women are so fond of the rattle of your own tongues that you never can let a man have his say!' he cried, bringing down his hand so heavily on the table that the tea-things danced again. 'I repeat, this money is such a trifling sum that it seems really absurd for a man whose time is as precious as mine to interfere in the matter; still, for the sake—'

'Uncle Gregory,' said Prue, summoning her

courage for the third and last time, 'I am
really—'

The look she encountered was so withering
that I almost expected to see her turn into stone,
straight away. What were the words that accompanied it I cannot say, for at this moment
there was a knock at the front-door. I rose, and,
despite the 'Et tu, Brute!' look cast after me by
Prue, hurried out of the room. Instinctively I
felt that help was at hand; and when, a moment
after, I returned and ushered in Father O'Connor,
I thought Prue would have burst out into a *Te
Deum* there and then.

Not so uncle Gregory, who was a bigoted
Protestant, and who disliked priests immensely,
with that unreasoning dislike now happily, in a
great measure, a thing of the past. His dislike
to the Catholic religion had probably not been
diminished by the conversion of his two sisters
Prue's mother and mine. I may, however, add
that his regrets on the subject were generally
upon the score that his mother did not know
what was going to happen when she made her
will, or she never, he averred, would have excluded her orthodox son to the benefit of her
heterodox daughters. Those who knew dear old
grannie best, with her love for her girls; and
her large-hearted liberality, were of a different
opinion.

'I suppose this gentleman, if he's going to

stay, has no objection to our continuing our business, as I've come over on purpose,' said uncle Gregory, breaking an awkward pause that had followed an introduction hardly less awkward, and glaring wrathfully at the intruder.

'By no means, Mr. Farley,' said the priest; 'but do you know, I am afraid you have had your journey for nothing. Miss Miller's money is all gone.'

'Gone!' repeated uncle Gregory.

'Yes, gone! Taken to itself butterfly wings and departed, leaving behind it only a chrysalis skin, in the form of an old woollen stocking!'

'Gone!' repeated uncle Gregory, drawing himself up, every vein swelling with offended majesty, 'and without consulting me?'

'My dear sir, you must forgive her; she did mean to consult you, but three different opportunities occurred one after another of investing the money, all so desirable, all promising such glorious interest, that she found it impossible to resist them.'

Uncle Gregory evidently refused to believe his ears. To do him justice, he had really intended investing the money to advantage, and with no other benefit to himself but that tribute to his superior sagacity that his pomposity always exacted from those he condescended to assist. To think that his own niece, a mere chit of a girl, should presume to despise his proffered advice, and that a Roman Catholic priest should coolly dare to tell him so, was rather too much.

'Impossible to resist them, indeed!' he exclaimed at length. 'Well, I have always known women to be fools, but I never thought one could have been such a fool as Prudence Miller has shown herself to be. Well, sir, may I ask the particulars of this investment, which Miss Miller's profound sagacity, seconded no doubt by yours, has found so desirable?'

'You may, Mr. Farley, though let me tell you my counsel was never given, for it was never asked; but each investment had my heartiest approbation when I heard of it.'

'Your approbation, indeed! a fat lot of value there was in that, I should think,' growled the old man, scowling down superciliously on the somewhat diminutive form of our young parish priest. 'Well, now go on, tell me about the investment. Some of those rascally new companies, I suppose, with their eight and ten per cents.'

'No; a very old one, on the contrary, Mr. Farley; for the company of Sorrowers, Sufferers, and Sinners (not limited) is old as mankind itself. Nor does it offer eight or ten per cent; but it promises an interest thirty, sixty, or a hundredfold, and gives as its security the Word of God Himself. Prudence Miller, as you know, had only twenty pounds; listen, and I will tell you how they went. The first investment saved an aged widow from penury and misery; the second, under the blessing of God, rescued a young girl from the very jaws of death, and restored her once more, bright and healthy, to her mother's arms, to labour for that mother's upport. What the third investment was I may not say; but there is a soul to-day living, we may fairly hope, in the grace of God, and longing to dedicate itself especially to His service, who, but for that gold and its timely help, might have been, and probably would have been, grovelling in the sin and misery that surely track the path of the desperate. Believe me, Mr. Farley, every penny of every pound has had its own peculiar blessing and reward; and although you are an old man, and think very little of the words of a young one like me, you may believe me when I say that your niece has acted well and wisely. For, all unworthy though I be, I am God's own minister, and as such I have already stood at many a death-bed, and seen the end of many a worldly investment, many a human scheme. On the strength of the experience I have gained in such scenes, will you let me say one little word more?'

'Certainly, sir, as many as you like, if you will first allow me to reach my hat.'

Of course it was handed to him, and, planting it defiantly on his head, he strode out of the room and down-stairs. A moment later the banging of the house-door told us that uncle Gregory's dreaded visit was at an end.

It is many a long day since all this happened, so long that Prue and I are beginning to turn gray. We are living together in her little cottage at Handley; for I went to her directly my good old aunt's death left me my income, and enabled me to give up my music-pupils. Prue too has had a legacy left her, and that by no less a personage than uncle Gregory. He never saw her, never spoke of her, until he lay upon his deathbed, when he suddenly asked for his will, and added a codicil to it in her favour. The letter that brought us the news of his death conveyed also the astonishing intelligence that the old man had left Prudence twenty pounds a year.

For fifteen years the old gray stocking had been hanging empty on its nail, but when that letter came I quite agreed that Prue need no longer think of saving. I was obliged to put my phrase in that form, because, between you and myself, dear reader, she had done nothing else towards it all that time; so we took it down, and having paired with the one I still possessed, sent the two old stockings, thus strangely united after fifty years of separation, to the old gardener, Jacob Williamson, to keep him warm for the winter. So here ends all I know, or am ever likely to know, of the history of cousin Prue's stocking.

OLD ISAAC'S CHRISTMAS-BOX

Or ' Dominus probibebit.'

CHAPTER I.

THE CHRISTMAS GUEST; WHO HE WAS, AND WHY THEY ASKED HIM.

IT was Christmas-eve; that day when, even amid the shadow of its solemn fast, the heart seems to tingle already with the joy of the coming festival. On the second floor of a little London house, a young workman and his wife might have been seen sitting down to their frugal maigre dinner. Everything in the room was as brightly furbished up as any housekeeper could desire to see her goods and chattels at that festive season; and as the little wife herself was as neat as a new pin, the herrings well cooked, and the baby in the cradle as healthy as a baby could well be, we are sure our readers will agree with us that George Miller might consider himself a very fortunate husband. As we happen to know his sentiments on the subject, we may say that he did not think one more fortunate could be found in the whole width and breadth of London.

'Is Mrs. Miller at home?' asked a voice from the stairs.

'What's up now, I wonder?' exclaimed George.

'Please, Mrs. Miller, here's somebody wants you,' said the landlady, outside the door; 'somebody from Mrs. Gregory.'

'All right, thank you, ma'am!' answered George. 'I wish they would let folks eat their dinner in peace,' he added, in a *sotto-voce* growl.

'O, hush, George! please don't say that!' cried Bessie, springing from her seat, and holding up her finger; 'it's my money come at last.'

'What money?'

'Why, for that dress I made;' and Bessie, after a fancy dance of delight, putting on a sober countenance, tripped down-stairs.

'Yes, here it is, sure enough!' she exclaimed, reappearing after a few minutes. 'Here it is, at last; but too late to do what I wanted with it. I have been so disappointed about it. I meant to have spent it all in materials for Christmas presents for you and mother and Janey. It's quite three weeks since I sent the dress home, and it fitted perfectly, the servant says. Never mind; better late than never.'

'Certainly, better late than never; but why should not Mrs. Gregory have paid you at once? She has plenty of money,' said George, looking indignant.

'Ah, George, why don't rich people always pay their bills? I'm sure I don't know; it is a mystery to me, and I don't believe the wisest man in the world could give you the reason. I daresay I shouldn't have had it now, if I hadn't written to Mrs. Gregory yesterday, asking for it, and giving Christmas being so near as a reason for wanting it. My own money! just imagine that; for all the world as if I was asking for charity!'

'It's a shame; a downright shame!' cried George; 'such people ought to be exposed. Well, never mind, old girl, since it has come at last. As for the presents, I'm sure we shall all of us take the will for the deed.'

'Well, George, as it is too late for them, I think I may as well buy the Christmas dinner with it.'

'How much does it come to?'

'Only nine shillings; but then I have more than two shillings saved up in farthings. Would it be too much to spend on it, do you think?'

'No, little woman;' "Christmas comes but once a year," we must remember. By the time you have bought a small goose, the materials for the pudding, and a little fruit, you will not have much left. If there should be a trifle, wouldn't you like—'

'To give it to somebody poorer even than we are—isn't that what you were going to say?'

'It was.'

'There shall be a trifle, Georgy; as big a one as I can make it. Mother has promised me some of her home-made wine, so I sha'n't have to get that.'

'Just like her, good old soul; but I don't think it's fair, since we are to dine with her on New Year's-day. I hope, Bessie, we shall make her and Janey and my father happy to-morrow. Last year we were in the country at my aunt's; so this is the first Christmas you and I have ever played host and hostess, old woman. I hope it will be a jolly one.'

'It must be a happy one for me, as long as I have you and baby, and my mother, your father, and Janey,' said Bessie, gently stirring the cradle beside her; 'but I am afraid, George, it will be rather quiet for you. Wouldn't you like to ask some friend or other from the shop?'.

'They have all homes to go to.'

'But is there nobody else?'.

George hesitated. 'I would much rather have it as it is—a nice snug little family party. And yet there is one person I should very much like to ask. Ever since I was a boy it has seemed to me that, in honour of our Lord being homeless at Bethlehem, I should like everybody's Christmas dinner-party to include some person who has no friends to go to, somebody without a home.'

'O, yes; do you know any one?'

'Yes, I know an old man, a good pious old man, who has taken his Christmas dinner in a miserable little eating-house for years, and who never expects to eat one anywhere else, as long as he lives.'

'Do ask him, George.'

'But, Bessie, he is a very poor shabby old man—as shabby as a man can well be.'

'What of that? Anybody you like your father will like, and I'll answer for mother and Janey. Dear George, do ask him. Let him be my Christmas treat. I would rather give him a happy day than any other pleasure you could offer me.'

'God bless you, my girl! How exactly alike you and I think about everything, to be sure! What, ten minutes to one? I must be off, I have to go to Bermondsey. By the bye, how shall I be able to invite old Griffiths? I sha'n't be back till late, and he leaves work early this time of the year, and I haven't a notion where he lives.'

'Where does he work?'

'He is a sort of odd man at a large broker's near Leicester-square.'

'Not very far. Couldn't I go and ask him, when I run out for my marketings?'

'All right; give me a pencil, and I'll write the address. Tell him you are the wife of the young fellow that gets his snuff. He takes a particular kind, and I get it cheap for him. Good-bye, old woman; give us a kiss;' and jumping down the stairs three at a time, George started off to his work.

Very busy was Bessie after his departure. There were the dinner-things to wash, the hearth to clean, the baby to feed and tidy. Then extra plates and dishes and the best cups and saucers had to be reached down and dusted. So busy, indeed, was the little woman, that she was quite astonished when the twilight suddenly deepened, and she found it was positively getting dark. But darkness comes on apace at Christmas-time. Although it was only half-past four when Bessie and the baby started for their the marketings, the stars were already in the sky, gas blazing in the shops, and the rattling, jostling, bustling business of Christmas-eve had begun.

Some people will perhaps say that, if our friend Bessie had been really a good manager, she would have done the said marketings in the morning, and would have sat at home quietly in the evening with her needlework. To tell the truth, nothing would have pleased her better. If there was one hour she loved more than

Old Isaac's Christmas-Box. 173

another, it was the one when she sat with her husband's supper ready before the fire, listening for his footstep, while she stitched away for her own little reserve fund, with her baby rolling on the hearth-rug at her feet. But unfortunately, like the rest of us, Bessie Miller could not always have her own way. If you, dear Mrs. A, or Mrs. B., with plenty of money in your pocket, were to leave your shopping to be done at night, and not even begin to make your plum-pudding till Christmas-eve, we should agree with anybody who called you a bad manager; but if you had no money, how could you go to market, we should like to know? If George's master, and Mrs. Gregory, had been people with heads on their shoulders or hearts in the right place, they would have taken care, as many a benevolent employer does, that those they employed should receive their money in time to spend it to good advantage. As neither of these people thought or cared at all about the matter, little Mrs. Miller had to shop at an awkward hour, and to carry her baby out into the frosty night air.

But, thanks be to God, if our poor men's wives only know their own dignity they may shop late at night, even in the London streets, without molestation, and our poor men's babies, if only well wrapped up, can stand a pretty strong whiff of cold night air without danger of catarrh or inflammation. Happily, in this case there was plenty of dignity and plenty of good warm wraps. Bessie quite enjoyed the Christmas fun and brightness as she bustled in and out of the shops, while the baby cooed so bewitchingly at the gas-lights that a fatherly old butcher chucked it under the chin, and, busy though he was, seemed quite loth to see it go. He looked quite pleased when Bessie suddenly bustled back again, and asked him if he would mind taking charge of her basket while she went a little further.

We verily believe if she had tried to carry it poor little Bessie would have fainted under its weight, so amply had she stored it with good things. Relieved of her burden, she passed briskly enough along the streets between the Tottenham-court-road and Leicester-square. Once she paused in her way, and looked carefully at a narrow court. Having assured herself that it was the one she wanted, she threaded it in almost breathless haste (for it was not a pleasant locality in the dark), hurried up a rickety staircase, and tapped at a back-door. A very old woman opened it, and into her hand Bessie slipped all the change she had that evening received during her shopping. Before either the woman or her bed-ridden husband could thank her, with a kindly smile and Christmas greeting she had turned away, and in less than half a minute was once again on her way to Leicester-square.

The place was easily found. A dismal, dingy, rambling shop, whose owner seemed to combine —in a fashion peculiar to that region—the business of a broker with the pursuits of an antiquary. Articles of furniture, modern and antique, boxes of books, and pictures set on end, cumbered the doorway, and filled every available space in the interior; while in the window and on the counter were displayed china, statues, coins, old jewelry, and other articles of *virtù* of greater or less value. Dimly lighted at the back, with neither dealer nor customer in sight, it almost seemed as though its inhabitants, whoever they might be, had forgotten that such a blessing as Christmastide was in existence. As our little Bessie alternately knocked and waited, wondering naturally why such valuables should be left unguarded, the strange thought stole into her busy little brain how much she would like to clean out the old place, and dress it with Christmas evergreens and candles. She was just considering who the guests should be after it was all done, when a sound arrested her attention, and, turning round, she discovered an old man in the act of putting up the shutters outside.

'I beg your pardon, sir,' said Bessie, hurrying out; 'are you Mr. Griffiths?'

Had a shot been fired behind his ear, he could hardly have looked more startled. No wonder; for the first time for many a long year he seemed to possess once more an identity of his own. Somebody wanted him.

'Yes, ma'am,' he said at length, looking thoroughly perplexed; 'that's my name. But it can't be me you're wanting,' he added, after a pause. 'It must be the master, Mr. Jacobs, and he's just gone.'

'No, no, Mr. Griffiths, I don't; it's you yourself, and nobody else,' cried Bessie, smiling. 'I'm the wife of George Miller. You know him, don't you?'

'Miller! George Miller! No, ma'am, I don't. It's a mistake—all a mistake!'

'No, it's no mistake. Don't you know the young man who gets your snuff for you?'

Griffiths's face brightened. 'And you're his wife? Then, ma'am, all I've got to say is, you've got a husband you may be proud of. Not that I ever knew his name before, and, what's more, I didn't know that he knew mine, nor where I worked. But I've known him, boy and man, for nearly ten years, by dining with him at the same table at the Catholic Temperance Rooms; and again I say, ma'am, you've got a husband to be proud of. He's one of the best-hearted young fellows in all London; and many's the one would say the same, I know, if they was here, for many's the one he has helped in his time with a bit of money or word of advice, I know.'

'Well, Mr. Griffiths, he wants to have the pleasure of your company to dinner to-morrow; so do I.'

'Company! dinner!' echoed the old man, perfectly aghast.

'Yes, for to-morrow; Christmas-day, you know. You will come, won't you?' she asked, looking coaxingly up into his face.

'No, no, no! I can't; it's all a mistake! If you weren't *his* wife I should think you were poking fun at me. I go out to dinner! Ha, ha, ha!'

'Why not, Mr. Griffiths, to the house of a friend you have known ten years? We are only poor people ourselves, and there will only be George and me, and his father, and my mother and sister. You know George and me already, and you'll soon get to know the others too.'

'Young woman,' said Griffiths, 'look at my coat, and look at it well. Does that seem fit for company? Well, I haven't another.'

'What of that? We don't ask people for the sake of their coats, Mr. Griffiths. My husband likes you, and wants you to come for your own sake only.'

'Then I'll come, and God bless you both! Going out to a Christmas dinner! Well, well;

that's something old and something new jumbled into one! Which is it, Isaac Griffiths, which is it? Well, my dear, give me the address, and tell me the time, and I'll make myself as tidy as I can and come. God bless you!'

CHAPTER II.

WHAT UNCLE ISAAC SAW BESIDES APPLES AND NUTS.

FIVE years had passed away, and once again Christmas had come to gladden the earth with its message of love and peace to men of goodwill. Once again children, grouped around doorways, were singing those quaint old carols that sometimes even yet send forth a note learned in the days of faith. Once again the shopkeepers were decorating their tempting stores; once again the people of London were shopping, cooking, regaling, and rejoicing; once again, too, it was Christmas for George Miller and his wife. But many changes had passed over the world during the last five years; and nowhere had changes come, more bitter or harder to be borne, than in their little home.

It was in the same spot, and just as clean and tidy, just as much a *home*, as ever; but plenty and prosperity had departed, and poverty, iron-griping poverty, reigned in their stead. It is easy to say how it had come about. A commercial crisis had ruined George Miller's master, and for months the poor young fellow had been out of work. He had spent time and money, and had almost worn out his clothes, boots, and patience in seeking it throughout the length and breadth of London, but all to no purpose; and now the Union or starvation seemed to stare him and his family in the face.

Bessie, his dear little loving Bessie, had come nobly to the fore, working early and late —sometimes at charing, sometimes at needlework. But, with three children under five, one a baby in arms, it had been sadly uphill work. One would hardly have recognised the once handsome young couple in the gaunt hungry-looking man and the sickly little woman who were standing that Christmas-eve, in earnest deliberation, a little apart from the children, by the window. Melancholy enough was the subject of it, seeing they were both looking down at a single sixpence that lay in George's palm, and saw in it all they possessed in the wide world for their Christmas dinner. Their conference was cut short by a tap at the door ; and as Bessie stepped forward to open it, George whipped the little coin into his pocket, as though fearful that its presence might betray the secret of his utter indigence.

The visitor was only our old acquaintance Isaac Griffiths. A little balder and more bowed, perhaps, than when he had stood at the shop-window, five years before, talking to Bessie Miller; but just the same meek, quiet, shabby little man that George had known him for fifteen years. He had come, as he promised, that Christmas-day, and so warm a friendship had grown out of the visit that for many a long day past uncle Isaac, as they loved to call him, had seemed almost part and parcel of the family.

'Uncle Ike! uncle Ike!' sang out a duet of baby voices, as the old man walked into the room holding up a couple of little cakes. George's brow cleared as he placed a chair, while Bessie, with an old Italian heater, raked the embers of the miserable fire together. 'Glad to see you, Mr. Griffiths. Cold day, isn't it? Take off your comforter, won't you? Wish I'd something to offer you,' said George.

'Couldn't take it, if you had, my boy; 'pon my word, I couldn't. I've only got five minutes; but I thought I'd like to look you up to see how things stand. Come along, little uns; one on each knee. Sit still, like good little birdies, while I talk to father. Cock-horse by and by. Nothing new, my boy, I suppose?'

George shook his head mournfully. 'No, uncle Isaac, nothing new; for poverty is old enough, I guess.'

'Yes, old, old, very old,' said Griffiths; 'as old as Bethlehem itself, eh, George?' he added, after a pause.

'Yes,' said George; 'and so, come what will, we mustn't grumble.'

'Well, and I must say it's not often that you do. You've acted like a Christian all the way through, my boy; and you will see in God's own time that He has not forgotten you.'

'I know that; still, it is hard to see—' The sentence was unfinished, save by a glance at the children on Griffiths's knee.

'It is hard, but the good time is coming, and we shall see it before long. Except to serve Mass, I never learned but one bit of Latin in my life, and that's a good bit. When I was a lad I kept company with a young girl named Susie Armstrong. She died in her teens, a beautiful saintly death; but I remember her just as brightly and freshly as ever. Well, she once worked me a book-marker, and on it she put two words that Father O'Callaghan chose for her—*Dominus providebit.*'

'What do they mean?'

'"The Lord will provide." I took them for the motto of my life, then and there; and though I have seen many, many a dark day since, I have always believed in them, and they have always come true. And so they will with you. See, George, it is old and worn out now, like me; but I thought this morning I would bring my old book-marker and hang it up here, so that you both might look at it, and get fresh courage, as I have done many a time.'

As he spoke he drew from his pocket a little slip of cardboard, adorned with a faded ribbon, and handed it to George. Tears stood in the young man's eyes as he fastened it above the mantelpiece with a pin, while Bessie, between weakness and emotion, fairly cried.

'It's all I have to give,' continued Griffiths. 'Mr. Jacobs only pays me five shillings a week, as you know; and yesterday he said I wasn't worth that. It's very certain I couldn't pay for rent and food and fire for less, so if he lowers me I must go to the workhouse. Perhaps he will, for I used to have six shillings, till he knocked off a shilling five years ago—the very afternoon Mrs. Miller first found me out. You see the Lord provided then; for if He let me lose a little in one way He has made it up over and over again in sending you to me, the only real friends I've ever had since the days of my youth.'

'I'm sure it's little enough we've been able to do for you, Mr. Griffiths,' said Bessie, as she took up an old pitcher and walked towards the door.

'Here, Bessie, give me that!' cried George almost angrily; 'a man with nothing to do can at least fetch up the water, I should think.'

'There goes one of the finest fellows in London, if London only knew it!' cried old Griffiths, following him with his eyes. 'Just you cheer up, Mrs. Miller; depend upon it this state of things can't last long. If only for George's kindness and goodness to a poor broken-down old creature like me, I know they can't, to say nothing of what he's done over and over again for others. Keep up your heart, there's a good dear soul; it's only a passing trial. The Lord will provide.'

'I've been thinking,' said George, reëntering the room with his pitcher, 'what a comfort it is that neither of the old folks—neither Bessie's mother nor my father—lived to see this day. I did hope, Mr. Griffiths,' he continued, 'that, as long as you and we lived, we should have eaten our Christmas dinner together. But there's little use in asking you this year, my good dear friend, for it's pretty clear we sha'n't have one.'

'But we will be together all the same, Georgy, my boy, if you'll have me. If it's only a crust of bread and a drop of tea; and I suppose we shall both have that. I'll bring what I have, and put it to yours; at any rate, we'll do our best to keep Christmas.'

'Only to think of this time last year!' said George. 'Never mind; we won't talk about that. There is no use in thinking of a good fire when one is out in the cold.'

At this moment a knock was heard at the door; the instant after it flew open, and a young girl neatly dressed in black, about nineteen years of age, stood in the doorway with outstretched arms. The little ones jumped off uncle Isaac's knee and rushed towards her, while the kindest welcome possible beamed on the faces of the elders.

'Janey, my dear, how good of you to come!' exclaimed Bessie. 'How did you possibly manage to get out on such a busy day?'

'Got forward with my work this morning, and asked leave for half an hour; so I've just no time to stop, for I've taken up so much of it already, getting these things—the shops are all so full. Look, Bessie, here's a trifle for your Christmas dinner;' and she handed her sister a basket, with a smile better imagined than described.

A trifle! What? Two nice plump rabbits, potatoes, onions, and a plum-pudding just ready for the pot, a trifle?—to say nothing of a paper bag full of apples, and another little one of nuts! Perhaps it was because it was only such a trifle that Bessie, instead of thanking her sister, hid her face on her shoulders, while George buried his in his hands. As for old Isaac, he stood at a little distance, surveying the scene like a man in a dream. Suddenly he seized Janey's two hands and shook them as though he never would leave off; then reaching his old hat, he planted it firmly on his head, and, without a word to anybody, hurried down-stairs, and off to his dingy quarters in Leicester-square.

It was Christmas-day, and myriads of footsteps were hurrying home from church to the happy firesides that awaited them, while those five joyous words, 'The compliments of the season!' uttered in every variety of note and key, rang through the frosty air. Walking alone, yet forming one of the living stream that had just turned out of a church in a side-street, with a step unusually brisk, an eye unusually bright, and an ear still tingling with the *Venite adoremus*, strode a little old man, poor and shabby enough, yet so clean and tidy in his poverty, so peaceful in his briskness, and so kindly withal, that even strange faces reflected back his smile, and wished him a 'Merry Christmas.'

We need not tell our readers that this old man was uncle Isaac; nor need we say whither he was bending his steps, nor with what an outcry of welcome he was received when he reached his destination. The dinner was only waiting his arrival to be dished up, and in less than ten minutes afterwards the rabbits and onion sauce, done to a turn, smoked on the board, flanked on one side by a dish of mealy potatoes, and on the other by a fine big cabbage, contributed by Isaac; while the pudding bubbled in the pot, as though it was tired of its prison, and asked to be taken up and eaten. There was very little of holiday trim about the room—for even holly costs money in London— and more than one dingy mark on the wall spoke of household treasures gone for bread. The clothes, too, of the whole party were poor in the extreme; yet so joyous were they all, nevertheless, that when the brightest ray of sunshine mid-winter could conjure up strayed in at the window, it was positively put to shame by the sunshine that was already beaming on their faces and flashing in their smiles. Many a *recherché* dinner was no doubt eaten that day in London; but we question much whether grace was as heartily said over any of them as George Miller said it over his little table, with its brace of boiled rabbits.

With such savoury viands to discuss, and dear aunt Janey's kindness to talk over, they were not afraid to think even of the Christmas-days gone by. For aunt Janey herself, to say nothing of her expected arrival at tea-time, was so sweet a subject of conversation that even the terrible changes made by death and poverty were gilded by the gladness of the present moment. At last dinner came to an end. Mother cleared away the things, and swept the hearth; and then they gathered round the bright little fire (for we

Old Isaac's Christmas-Box. 187

quite forgot to say in the right place that, at the very bottom of aunt Janey's basket, stowed away under a pot of jam, had been found two tickets, sent by Janey's mistress—one for coal and another for groceries). Very happy did George and Bessie look as they sat on one side of the fire hand in hand, and very contented looked old Isaac as he sat on the other, alternately smiling up at them and down at the little ones. Any one taking a peep at the scene would have seen at a glance that, though poverty had certainly come in at the door, just as certainly love had not flown out of the window. So little did they need any addition to their happiness that 'we verily believe, if it had not been for the little ones, aunt Janey's nuts and apples would have been forgotten altogether. As it was they were very soon called for; and while Bessie, after arranging them neatly on a couple of small blue plates which she had reached down from a high shelf, pared an apple for uncle Isaac, father roasted the chestnuts, burning his fingers and making such comical grimaces that even the baby laughed at the fun. Certainly aunt Janey's Christmas basket had been a success, and no mistake about it.

Even after the apples had been eaten and every nut had disappeared, they sat talking in the twilight—the baby asleep, and the two other children nestling on old Isaac's knee. At last

Bessie, remembering that Janey would soon be due, rose to get tea ready, and, after putting the sleeping baby into her husband's arms, lighted a candle and filled the kettle. There was not much to light up in that little bare room—certainly nothing, one would imagine, that such a constant visitor as uncle Isaac had not seen a score of times already. And yet, when the candle, after spluttering and quivering for a minute, gradually asserted its right to shine, and began to twinkle knowingly on the objects around it, as its light fell on the two little blue plates that had formed Bessie's dessert-service, a strange startled look stole over old Isaac's face. Little but the edges of either was visible, both being heaped up with apple-parings and nut-shells. But, putting the children gently down, the old man threw their contents on the fire, and, adjusting his spectacles, examined their patterns, their rims, and the maker's name, over and over again. This done, he placed them, one on the other, beside him on the table, took off his spectacles, and gazed abstractedly into the fire.

His ruminations were interrupted by the arrival of Janey, and a large amount of bustle and excitement caused thereby. Still the plates were not forgotten. When Bessie placed the tea on the table she naturally enough proceeded to remove them. Old Isaac, however, with a

Old Isaac's Christmas-Box. 189

look almost beseeching in its eagerness, prevented her doing so; and although a look of surprise passed over Bessie's face, she let him have his way, and, having placed a chair for her sister, seated herself at the little table and poured out the tea. For the rest of the evening everybody was so busy listening to Janey's sprightly chatter, especially to her account of the festivities going on at that moment at her master's residence, that the little blue plates were suffered to lie at uncle Isaac's elbow without further remark or molestation.

It was well they were so taken up with Janey, or certainly both husband and wife would have been sorely puzzled by uncle Isaac's strange demeanour; by the puckering of his forehead and the working of his lips, as he carried on an imaginary conversation, to say nothing of his unwonted silence; for, though by nature quiet in temperament, with the Millers uncle Isaac was generally as lively as the children themselves. But they did not observe his abstraction, any more than they noticed the flight of time. The clock actually struck ten before they thought it was eight. Aunt Janey started up and put on her bonnet; but as she had been told not to hurry back, quite another half-hour was taken up in good-byes, each intended to be the last, but each only the beginning of another fresh talk. At last she really was ready, though even then Bessie kept her waiting while she tied a comforter round the neck of George, who was to see her home.

'Good-night, uncle Isaac,' said Janey.

'Good-night, my dear. You'll sleep happy to-night, if anybody does, child. I may as well say good-night to you too, George, for I shall be gone before you get back. But stop a moment; I want to ask you something. Have you got any more of these 'ere plates?'

'No, only those two. They came to us with poor father's things.'

'You wouldn't sell them, I suppose?'

'Sell them? Well, I should be sorry to part with them, for they must have been in our family rather over than under a hundred years. Still, as times go, I really would sell them if they would fetch anything at all worth while. But then I feel sure they wouldn't; for, do you know, they are actually selling plates now, much bigger and better looking, for a penny each. So, you see, secondhand goods such as those are just worth nothing.'

'Yes, they are, down at our place. People buy them for curiosities. Suppose I could get you half-a-crown for them, eh?'

'I would be more than thankful, Mr. Griffiths. Why, man, half-a-crown in my Bessie's hands means dinner for all of us for the best part of a week. Of course I am sorry to see them go;

but they're not the first thing we've prized that has gone. The Lord only knows what will be the end of it. Six weeks' rent owing to-morrow, and not a penny to meet it with! But we mustn't think of these things to-night.'

'*Dominus providebit*,' said the old man. ' Look at the book-marker, and keep up your heart.'

' I will, uncle Isaac, I will. I say, my friend, there will still be a bit of picking left on the rabbits, so mind you look in to-morrow. Goodnight.'

Two minutes later they were gone, and two minutes later than that, with the blue plates carefully tied up in a handkerchief and stowed away under his arm, uncle Isaac departed likewise.

CHAPTER III.

UNCLE ISAAC MAKES A CALL IN MAYFAIR.

ABOUT eleven o'clock next day Isaac Griffiths might have been seen wending his way along Park-lane. Although poorly clad, as usual, he was quite as carefully smartened up as on Christmas morning, yet his face wore a very different expression; for an air of thought and anxiety had usurped the place of the joyous smile that we saw yesterday attracting the attention even of the passers-by; and although many a party of young people bent on enjoying their Bank-holiday crossed his path, he saw nothing of it all, but strode on rapidly, with a small parcel under his arm, like a man intent on business, and no mistake about it.

It was not until he stood before a row of houses, each a magnificent mansion, that he relaxed his pace, finally halting altogether in front of No. 10. After an anxious survey of the house, he seemed to summon his resolution, and, hastily descending the area-steps, knocked timidly at a door. The peals of laughter that came from within soon told him that the servants of the establishment, like everybody else, were keeping Christmas. It was not, indeed, until Griffiths had knocked several times that the door was at length opened by a boy in a striped jacket.

'Does Lord Mannering live here, if you please?' asked the old man respectfully.

'Yes, he do. Who do you want?'

'I want to see Lord Mannering himself.'

'O, I say!' ejaculated the boy, opening a pair of very round eyes.

'Yes, I want to see him very particularly indeed, for—'

'Well, I never!' cried the lad, looking over his shoulder. 'I say, Mr. Tompkins!'

A gigantic footman, all powder and dignity, came lazily forward.

'What is it, boy?'

'Please, here's a man says he wants to see his lordship. What am I to say to him?'

'Say to him! Why, shut the door in his face, to be sure!' replied the other, taking, as he spoke, a contemptuous survey of Isaac. 'Speak to his lordship, indeed! Stuff and nonsense! What do you suppose Lord Mannering could have to say to the likes of him? Now, my man, be off, if you please. The boy can't stay here all day—we're busy.'

'But I want to see Lord Mannering so very particularly—that is to say, if he doesn't mind my coming on a Bank-holiday.'

'Bank-holiday, indeed! What the dickens do you suppose Bank-holidays have to do with *hus?*' cried Mr. Tompkins, his emphasis increasing with his wrath. 'You must be precious green, first to come and ask for a nobleman as you might ask for Tom there, and then to talk as if we kept Bank-holidays, like you snobs. If you don't take yourself off, I'll see that somebody makes you;' and Mr. Tompkins closed the door with a bang, and carried his plush and powder to the servants' hall.

But though Isaac walked towards the steps, he did not ascend them, but stood with one hand on the iron balustrade, greatly perturbed in spirit, wondering if poor men ever were admitted to speak to lords, and, if so, how they managed it. As his corner was at some little distance from the door, nobody observed or interfered with him, although several visitors for the servants arrived, and were received with hearty words of welcome at the very door from which he had just been turned so ignominiously away. At last a dapper young baker, in a tremendous hurry to get through his morning rounds, rang furiously at the bell; and as he happened to be on very friendly terms with the first kitchenmaid, that young person answered the bell in person, all smiles and simpers. After bread enough to stock a small shop—at least, so it appeared to Isaac—had been carried in, and a large amount of flirtation carried on, the baker departed, waving his hand to the damsel, who looked after him with such a pretty happy smile on her face that Isaac once again plucked up his courage, and addressed her.

'I beg your pardon, ma'am; I don't want to be troublesome; but though the gentleman I just saw here said Lord Mannering wouldn't speak to the likes of me, I feel sure he would if he knew I came about some old china.'

'That's very likely; for since Lady Mary came back from France, all the family seem to have gone old-china mad. Who did you see?'

'The boy called him Mr. Tompkins.'

'O, Tompkins, was it? Great surly bear! I'm not surprised at anything he says, for he never speaks a civil word to anybody. Wait here a minute, my man, and I'll go and speak to the housekeeper herself.'

With a glance of gratitude in his meek gray eyes, old Isaac returned to his station at the steps. In less than five minutes his little benefactress returned, beckoned him in, and led him to the housekeeper's room, and that under the very nose of Mr. Tompkins himself, who glared fearfully at him as he passed, looking as though he longed to annihilate him. So bewildered, however, was the old man by this rapid turn of fortune that he hardly observed him, but followed Susan as she led the way, with steps almost as nimble as those of the young girl herself. So unaccustomed was our old friend to any but the simplest household arrangements, that it seemed hardly possible that the cozy handsome room, into which he was ushered, could belong to any one but my lord, or that the old housekeeper, seated in a stately armchair, with her rich black silk and heavy chain, donned in honour of expected guests, could be any lesser personage than my lady. But he was quite undeceived when another footman, the very facsimile of Tompkins, except his scowl, entered with a message that my lord would like to see the old man, and he actually found himself on his way to the library. Timidly he passed over carpets that felt like moss itself, amid stained windows that made him fancy himself in church; among silken draperies, statues, pictures, gilding, and flowers; the whole tempered by almost a summer warmth, and blended in such rich confusion that no wonder old Isaac's brain whirled with admiration.

What would the owner of all this splendour be like? was a thought that shaped itself in the old man's brain, even amid his bewilderment. He could not imagine. The problem was, however, both suddenly and pleasantly solved when he was ushered into a very large room, where sat an old white-headed gentleman, in gentleness, kindliness, and benevolence the very counterpart of old Isaac himself.

'Good-morning, my friend; I wish you a merry Christmas,' said the Earl pleasantly.

'Thank you most kindly, sir—my lord, I mean,' replied the old man; 'and very many of them.'

'You wish to speak to me, I am told?'

'Yes, my lord.'

'Very well; take a seat first.'

Isaac looked at the softly-cushioned chairs in their morocco coverings, and muttered a respectful dissent.

'Nonsense!' said the Earl; 'sit down. I know by experience that when men come to our time of life their legs are not what they used to be. When I have come up only half as many stairs as you have, I'm glad enough to get into the first chair I see. So sit down there out of the draught. You come about some old china, I'm told.'

'Yes, my lord; about these plates. It seems to me they're the same as the one you showed my master, Mr. Jacobs.'

'O, you are Mr. Jacobs' man, I see?'

'Yes, my lord.'

Just as Griffiths himself had examined the plates the night before, Lord Mannering examined them now, and seemed pleased with the result of his scrutiny. 'May I ask you to ring the bell?'

Isaac obeyed, and Tompkins entered, as subservient as any master could desire. Isaac could hardly believe he was the same man.

'Please to go to Lady Mary's boudoir, Tompkins, and fetch me that little blue plate off the wall by the Indian cabinet.'

'Yes, my lord.' Tompkins vanished, but quickly returned, and placed the plate on the table.

'Thank you. Wait a minute, Tompkins. The next time any person calls and asks for me, please to ascertain whether he comes upon business before you take upon yourself the responsibility of refusing me. That will do.

'Yes, yes, the very same,' said the Earl, when the discomfited Tompkins had withdrawn. 'Well, my friend, tell your master they are all right, and I will call and pay him. He knows the price promised. Five guineas each.'

'Please, my lord, those plates don't come from the shop; they belong to a friend of mine,' and uncle Isaac told the story of his discovery the night before.

Lord Mannering listened attentively, even though Isaac made digressions about the Millers, that certainly had nothing to do with the plates.

'I understand,' said the Earl. 'Then instead of paying Mr. Jacobs a visit, I must call on George Miller instead, eh?'

'Yes, my lord; but wouldn't your lordship like him to come here?'

'No; I would rather call upon him. Ten guineas seems a long price for such small articles, does it not?' said the Earl, smiling, and taking the plates again in his hand. 'The fact is, my daughter, Lady Mary, is a great admirer of this style of china; and as she is my only child, and a very good child, I am sometimes, I fear, extravagant in gratifying her little fancies. You have brought these just in time for her birthday tomorrow, and I am delighted to have them; but I must say I am glad the money is going into the pocket of a poor and deserving man. You say your friend is out of work. Has he been used to the country?'

'Yes, my lord; his father was a farmer all his life, until somebody advised him to take a milk-shop in London; and George understands cows, horses, and everything of the sort.'

'Is he steady?'

'As steady as an old horse, my lord. A really hard-working, God-fearing young man, and what's more, a teetotaller.'

'All right; tell him I will call and pay him his money the first time I go out.'

'May the Lord bless you for ever, my lord! O my God!' he continued, clasping his hands, and forgetting even Lord Mannering in his emotions; 'didn't I tell them the Lord would provide?'

'Of course He will, for He always does,' said the Earl solemnly.

'Yes, yes, my lord, always.'

'Good-bye, my friend, for the present,' said the nobleman, as Isaac rose from his chair, and fumbled for his old hat underneath it; 'you won't forget my message to your friend?'

The old man's smile was his only answer.

It was past one o'clock when uncle Isaac arrived at the Millers' little home, and dinner was ready and waiting. And a very nice little dinner it was, too; for out of the remains of yesterday's feast, and a little coarse beef, Bessie had made a dish that would have been appetising even to persons accustomed to daintier fare, and, doubly, trebly appetising to those to whom dinner had latterly been rather an exception than a rule. There was a strange look on Isaac's face when, after the usual salutations and a little playful scolding for being late, he took his place at the table. But neither George nor Bessie remarked it any more than his unwonted silence and preoccupied air. Both were too busy with the duties of the table and the children to observe it, and it was only when George turned to invite him to a second help that he saw the old man's plate was still almost untouched, and that uncle Isaac himself was far, far away, smiling and rubbing his hands in unmistakable glee.

'Uncle Isaac, you look pleased; but you must get on with your dinner, or it will grow cold. Come, a penny for your thoughts.'

'They are worth more than that, young man, I can assure you; but I shall not sell them till after dinner.'

'All right; then we will be quick and finish,' said George, 'though I shall have to owe the penny, I expect,' he added, laughing, 'for I don't believe there's as much left in the house.'

'Yes, George, three-halfpence,' said Bessie; 'don't make us out poorer than we are.'

In a very few minutes dinner really had come to an end, and Bessie cleared the table, while the little ones minded the baby in a corner.

'Now, uncle Isaac.'

'Well, my boy, I was only thinking that this was Boxing-day, and saying to myself we ought to have our Christmas-boxes.'

'So we ought, and no mistake about it; but as it's very certain we sha'n't, I don't agree with you that your thought is worth the last penny in the house, and more.'

'Yes, it is, and you will say it is presently. If you could have your choice, what would you have for a Christmas-box, Mrs. Miller?'

'A whole ton of coals, I think, uncle Isaac. It seems to me the cold is harder to bear than anything else, such weather as this.'

'Money to pay the rent we owe, I should say,' said George. 'I think it is even easier to bear the cold than to feel one has no right to the very roof that shelters him.'

'Rent and coals! Is that all? Times must indeed be hard when two young creatures like you can think of nothing prettier or smarter, by way of Christmas-boxes, than rent and coals,' said uncle Isaac, with tears in his eyes. 'Well, my children, you shall have them both, and many, many things more, I promise you; and you know uncle Isaac wouldn't tell you a lie. George, my man, I have sold your little blue plates.'

'Blue plates!' echoed Bessie, who, like her husband, was growing pale with excitement.

'Yes; listen, and I will tell you all about it. A few months ago Lord Mannering, a very rich nobleman, came to our place with a little blue plate, which he showed the master, promising to pay very handsomely for any he could get like it. Mr. Jacobs tried everywhere, but it was of no use; the ware is so rare now, it is almost impossible to get it. I was out when Lord Mannering came, but I saw the plate often, for we had it some days at the shop. The instant I saw those two plates last night I felt almost certain they were the same; but I was afraid to speak, for fear I might be wrong and only disappoint you. I was not wrong; thank God, I was not wrong, for I took them this morning to Lord Mannering, and he bought them for ten guineas. Isn't that a Christmas-box worth having?'

Isaac's voice, that had been growing husky, now fairly broke down; Bessie's whole frame shook with stifled sobs; while even George could only wring his old friend's hand in speechless gratitude.

'I wanted his lordship to let me send you to him,' continued Isaac, as soon as he had recovered his composure, 'but he said he should much prefer calling here and paying you himself. But you needn't look so frightened, Mrs. Miller, for if ever there was a good, kind, sweet-spoken gentleman on this earth, it is Lord Man—'

There was a gentle tap at the door. George mechanically opened it, and before any one had even time to feel discomposed the subject of their conversation stood before them.

It was not by any means for the first time in his life that Lord Mannering now found himself under a working man's roof. As the owner of a large estate in one of the midland counties, his love for his tenantry was almost the affection of a father for his children, and their welfare and happiness had been one of the favourite studies of his life ever since his accession to the estate. Heart and head had both been brought to bear upon the great question of master and man; and as no one knew better than he the value of the working classes, so no one knew better how to win their confidence and esteem. Throughout the width and breadth of his immense estate he and his family were almost idolised for their individual love of every man, woman, and child upon it. Before he had been seated five minutes in George Miller's little room, the whole party were talking to him as urestrainedly as though they had been born and bred in his lordship's own village of Mannering.

'And you really would like a country life, you think, Mr. Miller?'

'Indeed we would, both of us, my lord. We were born among the green fields, and many's the time we have regretted that the children shouldn't even know what they were like. Haven't we, Bessie?'

'Do you know anything about the cultivation of flowers?'

'Yes, my lord, I do, and vegetables as well. I always kept the garden at home; and, though I say it, there wasn't one anywhere about to beat it. Even here, my lord, I rear as many as I can, and I have a fine show in the summer.'

'That he has, my lord,' chimed in Isaac.

'Well, listen to me. I am one of the directors of the new railway that is to pass through Mannering; and, as it has been necessary to build the station in full view of the Hall, I have taken pains to make a very pretty little place of it. There is a flower-garden attached, that I shall expect to see kept in perfect order; and I have given a good piece of land at the back for a kitchen-garden; so, even if the trains are few, it will be the station-master's own fault if his time hang heavily on his hands. Now, as I have paid a large share of the expense of all this, the company have asked me to choose the station-master myself; and from what I see of you, and from what you tell me concerning your capabilities, I fancy you are the very man to suit me, if you care to accept the situation. I do not know exactly what the salary is to be; but it will, I know, be sufficient to maintain an industrious family in comfort. What do you think of the idea?'

For an instant, to the Earl's surprise, there

was a dead silence; the next, with a voice strong in its determination even in the moment of temptation, the young man replied, 'My lord, I can never thank you enough for your kind offer. The place is exactly what I should wish for—before everything else. But, my lord, I am afraid you would not like to have us when I tell you one thing.'

'What is that?' asked the Earl, looking strangely perplexed.

'My lord, we are Catholics.'

'Is that all? Well, I am a Protestant myself, but I am glad to have Catholics about me, for I have always found that if Catholics go regularly to their "duties" (as they call them), there are no better servants in the world. We have a nice little church on the estate, and a dear good man for a parish priest—a better I have never known; and I see him often, for we are capital friends. There is a good school, too, for the children, so, you see, your religion is quite safe. I will give you a couple of days to consider my offer. At the end of that time I should like to know whether or not you will accept it.'

Would he accept it? If he did not go down on his knees then and there, in gratitude to his benefactor, it was because George Miller was not the man to make a scene. His lordship had only to look at the man's overflowing eyes to see that he need say no more about the two days' consideration.

'And now, my good friend Mr. Griffiths,' said Lord Mannering, turning to Isaac, 'I have a word to say to you, and, I am afraid, rather an unpleasant one. On my way hither, my carriage was stopped by a cab-horse in front of it slipping down, and while my coachman waited, who should I see on the side-walk but your master, Mr. Jacobs. I had no idea I could do you any harm by detailing our little transaction of this morning; so I beckoned him to the window, and told him I had managed to get my plates, and how. He was perfectly civil, but I never saw a man look more angry than he did when I mentioned you. Of course, you had an unquestionable right to act as you did, but I suppose he thinks you should have sold the china to him. I am afraid he will be very angry with you.'

Old Isaac's face looked the picture of dismay.

'Will he turn you off, do you think?'

'I am afraid he will, my lord.'

'And be only too glad of the excuse, my lord,' added George. 'He has reduced our poor friend's wages almost to starvation-point already, on account of his age; and he is always telling him a boy would be twice as useful to him.'

'What do you do for him?' asked the Earl.

'Clean pictures, my lord, and frames, and rub

up the old brasses, and suchlike, besides going the errands.'

'Do you understand how to clean pictures properly?'

'Yes, my lord; I was brought up to the trade.'

'Would you like to change masters?'

The only answer was a stare of utter astonishment.

'Because, if you would, I will take you into my own service. I have a very large collection of pictures and curios, that cost me no end of money every year to keep in order. Now, I am ready to engage you at ten shillings a week to look after them. Sometimes I shall want you up here at my house in London, but only occasionally, for I have nothing here of much value. My real collection is at Mannering, and your home will be there. You will easily find board and lodging in the village.'

'With us,' whispered Bessie, furtively taking the old man's hand, and stroking it affectionately.

'Then I think all is settled,' said the Earl, rising to depart. 'Nothing remains but to get your reference; and if this is satisfactory, as I feel assured it will be, I will write and tell you when and how to get to Mannering. You must all be settled down by the end of next month, for the railway opens on the 1st of February.'

Many years have passed since the events recorded in our little story, and George and Bessie Miller are getting quite old married people. All has gone well with them, for their children are happy and thriving, and as for the station, everybody admits it is the prettiest on the line. The whole family are great favourites at the Hall, where the eldest girl is already installed as kitchenmaid under Isaac's old acquaintance Susan, now the buxom, good-tempered Mannering cook. As to old Isaac himself, so many latent talents has he developed, and so indispensable has he grown to the Earl, that his lordship long since dubbed him his 'right-hand man.' Lady Mary has never married, having refused all offers for her dear old father's sake. She is especially fond of Isaac, who returns her partiality with childlike devotion. He has told her all his history, even the story of the little bookmarker; and we have heard a rumour—though we cannot vouch for its truth—that Lady Mary Mannering, who is both a poetess and a musician, is about to publish a sacred song, the title of which is to be 'Dominus providebit.'

www.ingramcontent.com/pod-product-compliance
Lightning Source LLC
Chambersburg PA
CBHW020828230426
43666CB00007B/1141